THE COLLIERIES OF DURHAM VOL.2

DAVID TEMPLE

Copyright: D. Temple / J. T. Tuck
Printed and published by TUPS Books, 30, Lime St. Newcastle upon Tyne, NE1 2PQ.
Tel.No: 0191 2330990 Fax: 0191 2330578
ISBN 1 901237 01 X

This book is dedicated to the men of the Mines' Fire and Rescue Brigades

FOREWORD

The Durham miners owe a debt of gratitude to the author of this book who has researched the history of Chopwell, Dawdon, Easington, Mainsforth, Greenside and the South Moor group of collieries. He has chronicled the development of the collieries and the struggle of the miners and their families.

The introductory history captures the solidarity, the stubbornness and resolve of the local branches of the union to influence their destiny and to improve the quality of their lives despite the overwhelming pressure from governments, coalowners and on occasions their own union.

In 1913 one in three of the working population of Durham worked in the mining industry. They made an enormous contribution to the wealth of Britain and received little, in social and economic terms, for their sacrifice. The dependence of Durham upon coal shaped the nature of our communities and that of Durham people. This book highlights the role that these miners and their families played in times of tragedy and confrontation and gives the reflections of some who played a part.

Today the villages of Durham face a similar struggle to that experienced in the past. A struggle against unemployment and low pay with all their social consequences. The erosion of the Welfare State, so patiently built by the people depicted in this book, compounds the problems. But the principles remain the same - 'Unity is strength'. 'An injury to one is an injury to all.' We are bound by a common bond to build a better life for all, an inheritance so richly deserved by the sons and daughters of the Durham miners.

David Guy
President of the North East Area NUM

ACKNOWLEDGEMENTS

This is the fourth book that has been produced as a result of the close collaboration between myself and James T Tuck. Without Jimmy this book could not have been written.

I am particularly indebted to George Ottwell of Easington for his description of the courageous role played by the rescue brigades in the Easington disaster of 1951. Also Billy Stobbs of Easington for providing photographs of the 1984/85 strike.

George Muncaster for his patience in explaining to me the complex development of the South Moor group of collieries and his help in providing me with a number of invaluable photographs.

Alan Kennedy, Alan Johnson and Frank Shaw and Jackie Hall of Dawdon for all their help over a number of years for the chapter on Dawdon colliery. Also Easington District Council.

I am grateful to C. Downs, J. Carrick, J. Hamilton, C. Stout and C. E. Mountford for their help in providing photographs without which this book would be very much the poorer.

Finally my thanks are due to all my colleagues at TUPS for their skill and dedication that has produced this book.

PREFACE

It is now four years since the last colliery in Durham closed and with incredible speed all visible traces of mining have been wiped from the face of the county. All that remains is some open spaces where alongside a pulley wheel sunk into a concrete plinth a few new business units have been erected.

The thousands of miners who once earned their living thousands of feet below the ground are dispersed throughout the county, standing guard in shopping precincts, delivering pizzas or driving taxis. For many others the pigeon-loft and the leek-trench, once diversions from hard labour, are now a full-time occupation.

There is talk of changing the names of villages and discarding the affix 'colliery' as if by just changing the name we make a break with the past and usher in a new and prosperous era.

The spirit of our mining heritage does not reside in visible remains, monuments, however grand, or place names, but in our selves, in our values and in our memories. I hope the collieries of Durham Vol. 2 goes a little way to keeping those memories alive and to passing on what is a great history to another generation who have many problems to contend with.

David Temple

CONTENTS

HISTORY

1869 - 1913

As Prussian forces battled their way over the coalfields of Alsace and Lorraine and laid siege to Paris the mineowners of Durham were busily taking advantage of the rising price of coal stimulated by the disruption of supplies from Europe. Such was the disruption that by 1872 Durham coal had everything going for it, high prices and rising demand.

Shafts were being sunk to Durham's seams as fast as sinkers could be found to sink them; The Victorian County History gives us an insight into the extent of the development.

In the year of 1872 :

No. 2 shaft, Florence pit, Kepier colliery, was sunk from the surface to the Busty seam.

The Pelton New Winning, Newfield was commenced and sunk from the surface to the Busty seam.

Cowen's Pit, Blaydon Burn colliery, was sunk from the surface to the Brockwell Seam.

Witton Pit Charlaw colliery, was sunk from the Hutton to the Busty Seam.

No. 1 shaft, Chilton colliery was commenced on 29 February, and sunk to the Main coal seam.

A series of borings was put down from the surface on the Holmside Royalty, proving the Hutton Seam and upper coals, and another series of boreholes in the vicinity of Woodlands colliery, proving the Brockwell Seam.

Boring operations from the surface were also in progress in the vicinity of Crake Scar

Colliery, Cockfield, and others by Coulson on the Winston estate, proving a coal seam 30in thick, lying just above the Gannister Beds.

Commenced to sink the New Pit, Trimdon

Willian Crawford, General Sectretary, DMA 1872-90

1

First Miners Hall. North Rd. Durham.

Grange Colliery, from the surface to the Busty seam.

East Howle Colliery commenced to sink and was put down to the Brockwell Seam.

In this year there were seventeen Guibal ventilators at work in South Durham alone. Air compressing plant was erected at Ryhope and at North Hetton Collieries for working underground , machinery, coal cutters etc'

Great advances had been made in mining technique. Steel could now be manufactured in great quantities by the new Bessemer converters. Central to this process was the manufacture of coke, increasing further the demand for good coking coal. The collieries of Durham, the laboratories of machine innovation, was itself the greatest beneficiary of this powerful new material. Stronger and more efficient steam engines could be built powering, better pumps and more efficient fans. Although the pick was to last in most pits well into the 20th century, compressors were being developed to power pneumatic cutting machines.

This was the period of gestation for electromagnetism, which would transform Michael Faraday's laboratory experiment linking the new phenomena of electricity to mechanical movement and produce, in time, the electric motor. By the turn of the century the mining engineer would be able to transmit power down the mine by cable to huge haulage motors.

While machinery was developing apace, painfully slow progress was being made in the field of mining safety. After the horrendous disaster at New Hartley Hester colliery in 1862, where 204 men and boys perished for want of a second means of egress, public opinion prevailed and a Bill was passed through Parliament requiring two shafts at all new mines. Furnace ventilation had reduced the instances of explosion and remained the principal method of ventilation throughout the 19 th century. But disasters still occurred all too frequently and the almost daily carnage due to roof falls continued as production was traded for safety.

A new Pitmen's Union, The Durham Miners Association (DMA), had been formed in 1869 and was making steady progress.

Old Tommy Ramsey, hero of the 1844 strike, had come in from the cold. This faithful unionist who had trudged from village to village, crake in hand, expounding the cause of unionism, sleeping under hedgerows, shunned by miners fearful of

First deputation from the Durham Miners Association to the Coal Trade Office, Newcastle upon Tyne, February 17, 1872

Back row: N Wilkinson (Treasurer), W. H. Patterson (Vice-President), M. Thompson T. Ramsey G. Jackson, J. Forman

Front Row: W. Askew, W. Crawford, J. Handy T. Mitchinson

the consequences of being seen in his company, was now given a job as a union agent and a salary to go with it.

This new union was led by men with missionary zeal, Primitive Methodist men who had put God on the side of the miner. Their God was a God of social justice. Not to be a member of the union was to deny the will of God. It was a sin. This new union was carving out its place at the centre of Durham village life, a place it would hold unrivalled for more than a hundred years.

These men believed that if the union was strong then the leaders were strong and the employers would then listen to reason and reason would prevail.

For Crawford, Foreman and Patterson Capital and

Labour were two noble beasts each having their place. If they were in conflict with each other then a lesser beast, the consumer, would take advantage. If they sat down and reasoned together both would benefit. This was their fervent belief.

The mineowners of Durham had never recognised a union amongst pitmen. Their response to strikes had in the past been violent, relying on the army and a rag-bag force of thugs recruited from the big cities to smash any resistance in the coalfield. But in 1872 they had much to lose and so formed themselves into the North of England United Coal Trades Association and decided to give reason a chance.

When in 1872 this new association invited the DMA to the negotiating table there was no hesitation.

The first meeting took place in February of that year and the union requested an advance in wages of 35% for all men working underground. 20% was granted. Later that year the owners agreed that the hated yearly bond, that had kept the pitmen of Durham in a state of semi-serfdom, would be abolished.

The new miners' union was not without its internal problems. The DMA leaders favoured a centralised union based on full-time agents. They far preferred to be given the power to negotiate with the employers and to reach a settlement without further consultation with the ordinary miner. If the paternalism of the employer was expressed in the occasional feast when opening a new mine, the building of a church or school, or just the owner's wife playing Lady Bountiful around the village, then the union leaders had their own brand of paternalism - the paternalism of a Father who knows what's best for his children.

The DMA, however, had grown out of local associations based on particular collieries and often grouped around the election of checkwieghmen. The right of the men to elect one of their number to check the weight of coal raised was granted by an Act of Parliament pre-dating the formation of the DMA. This legislation was further strengthened in 1895, when it was amended to allow men to be elected who were not necessarily employed at the colliery and therefore free of the influence of the owners. Much of the disruption of the collieries had been provoked by the miners' well-founded belief that he was constantly being cheated by the company wieghman.

The economic life of the village centred on the pit. The local lodge of the union was the only means through which all the frustrations of day-to-day life could be resolved. These village communities exercised a gravitational pull away from the centre, preventing lodges from becoming satellites of the Durham leadership. They had their own orbit around the various communities they represented.

This antagonism between the DMA leaders and the miners they represented erupted into open revolt the moment the trade took a down-turn. The Franco-Prussian war and the disruption of European coal supplies had created a coincidence of interest between owners and men that was short-lived. It was one thing to allow the leaders to negotiate advances in a rising market; it was something else to allow them to negotiate reductions.

In April 1874 the owners demanded a reduction in wages of 25% and the Durham leadership recommened that the union offer a reduction of 10%. A coalfield conference accepted the recommendation but when the decision was conveyed to the men they were incensed.

J Wilson, himself one of the Durham leaders, in his History of the Durham Miners Association was to record:

'The spirit of revolt was rampant throughout the county amongst the members of the

Miners Association. Circulars were sent out by District Councils, in which the Executive Committee was held to ridicule.'

Mass meetings were held throughout the county. In some cases as many as 10,000 gathered to reject the offer and condemn the leadership, but on this occasion the Durham leaders finally prevailed and after a week of sporadic strikes a reduction of 10% was narrowly agreed.

Five years latter in 1879 it was a different story. After a series of reductions the owners demanded a further 20% reduction. To reach an agreement the Executive asked for 'full and uncontrolled power' but were denied this by the membership. The newly formed Federation Board representing Miners, Enginemen and Deputies offered seven-and-a-half per cent and the owners reply with an offer of ten per cent reduction underground and seven-and-a-half per cent at bank. The Board recommended acceptance of this new offer. John Wilson again records the response.

'...there arose fierce agitation in the county and on every hand mass meetings were held protesting against the terms. As is the case in matters of this kind, orators vehement if not polished sprang up from every quarter, whose stock-in-trade consisted of foul epithets which they hurled at the Committee and Federation Board. So desperate was the situation that certain of the Committee were in fear and came into public view as little as possible.'

Wilson, himself a member of the committee, explains how he was affected by this disscent. As Chairman of the Wheatley Hill Lodge Wilson marched to a mass meeting held on the Sands at Durham. As they marched on to the field the first word that was heard was *'There's one of the ——; let's put him in the river!'*. The crowd surged towards him and there was a great struggle. When it was at its height a large miner fell on to the big drum of the brass band, which

W. H. Patterson

ruptured with an enormous bang. The cry went up *'They are firing on us.'* Panic set in and the crowd stampeded for cover, leaving Wilson dishevelled but unharmed.

The miners and their union were now in a familiar situation. The coal trade was at the bottom of a trough and the owners were in a strong position and they knew it. The miners demanded arbitration but the owners refused, threatening to lock out all men who would not work for an increased reduction of 15%. Again the Executive advised caution but the membership were adamant and voted to strike. They finally return to work seven weeks later on a reduction of eight-and-three-quarters per cent. A further one-and-a-quarter per cent reduction was added in July by arbitration.

Despite the many rebuffs from both men and management the leaders of the DMA never tired in their quest for the elusive peace between men and masters. For a full 12 years they attempted to regulate wages by tying advances and reductions to the fluctuating price of coal, a system known as the sliding scale, but it always broke down in the end. Reason could never overcome the simple fact that the owners desire to defend profits was equal to the pitmen's defence of wages. The owners could not control the market and the Durham leaders could not control the men.

The union's activity was not confined to the question of wages. In 1880 in a rising market they turned to the question of hours of work and secured an agreement restricting a hewer's shift to one of not more than seven hours bank to bank. They also secured the agreement that no colliery would raise coals for more than ten hours per day. Although other underground classes of men continued to work ten hours this was an astounding success which was to be jealously guarded over the years.

This advance was not without its problems. Since the hewers represented the most numerous and influential section of the union, the union were obliged to oppose the struggle for a legal eight-hour day in fear that if it became law the owners would increase the hours of work for hewers. A further problem would arise in that if the men working ten hours were reduced to eight then it would mean the introduction of a further shift and the subsequent drawing of coals over a longer period than ten hours. They were at pains however to explain that they were not opposing other classes of workmen achieving an eight-hour day, but that they believed that this should be achieved by trade union activity and not by legislation.

It was this question of hours that was the principal reason why apart from a brief spell between 1892 an 1893 the DMA remained outside the Miners Federation of Great Britain (MFGB) until 1908. It was in this same year that an Act of Parliament was passed restricting the hours of labour of all underground men to a shift of not longer than eight hours. While the DMA reached agreement with the owners that the hewers hours would remain unchanged at between six-and-a-half and seven hours depending on the colliery, the owners of some collieries changed the shift pattern to accommodate the shorter shift for putters and back-bye workers. A wave of strikes affected collieries in 1910 and during a riot at Horden colliery the miners burnt down the club that the owners had built.

The decision of the DMA to join the MFGB effectively united British miners into one

John Wilson

organisation which was a federation of independent trades unions. In 1912 this new unity resulted in the first united national strike of miners. Their aim was to achieve a national minimum wage.

At a time when coal was virtually the sole source of power the effect on the country was devastating. The Asquith Government quickly passed a Bill legislating for a minimum wage but one based on area agreements. This fell short of the miners' demand for a national minimum but vacillation within the leadership of the MFGB, a weakening in the Midlands coalfield and an unexpected collapse of the vote to continue the strike in the militant Welsh coalfield brought the strike to an end on the basis of this partial solution. There is no doubt that the Government was concerned that a national minimum would have a uniting influence across the coalfields and lead to a truly national union as opposed to a looser alliances of federated unions. The result of this action brought a new word in the vocabulary of Durham miners, 'the mini'.

By the turn of the twentieth century the Durham coalfield was entering its final phase of development. Production peaked in 1913 when 166,000 men were employed in the industry in the county of Durham.

The technique of freezing the area around a new sinking enabled coal companies to sink shafts through the limestone that concealed the coal measures in the east of the coalfield. The herculean struggle against the waters of the sand feeder that had dominated the sinking of Haswell, Hetton, Wearmouth and Murton collieries in the first half of the nineteenth century had deterred further attempts to go beneath the limestone. With this new method at hand, Dawdon, Easington and Horden collieries were sunk. These massive coal-producing machines employed thousands of

John Foreman, President DMA, 1872-1900

hewers working the high seams under the North Sea. While these giants of modern mining were constructed in the east the high quality of the west of Durham coking coal kept miners employed in narrow seams in primitive conditions that would change little until they closed well into the twentieth century.

Durham's unique character had been fashioned out of the production of a single commodity which in 1913 reigned supreme. The coalfield was now poised to begin its long and painful decline.

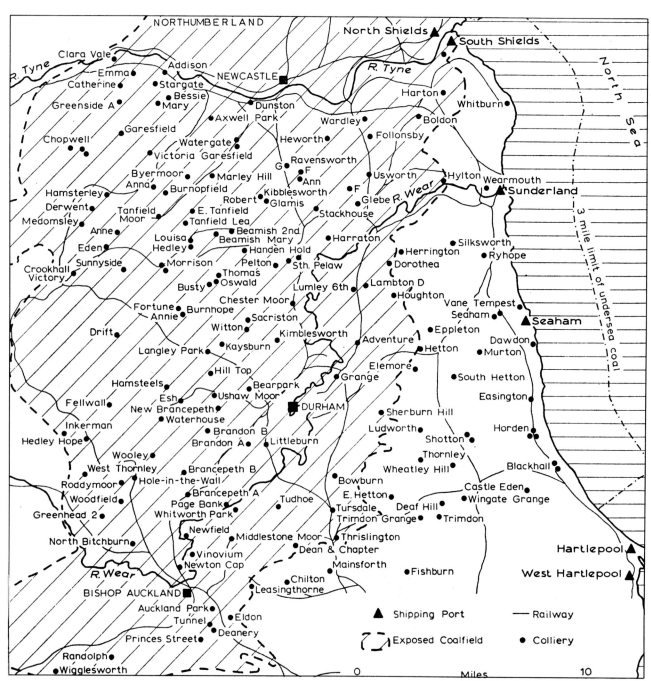

Durham coalfield showing collieries operating in 1942

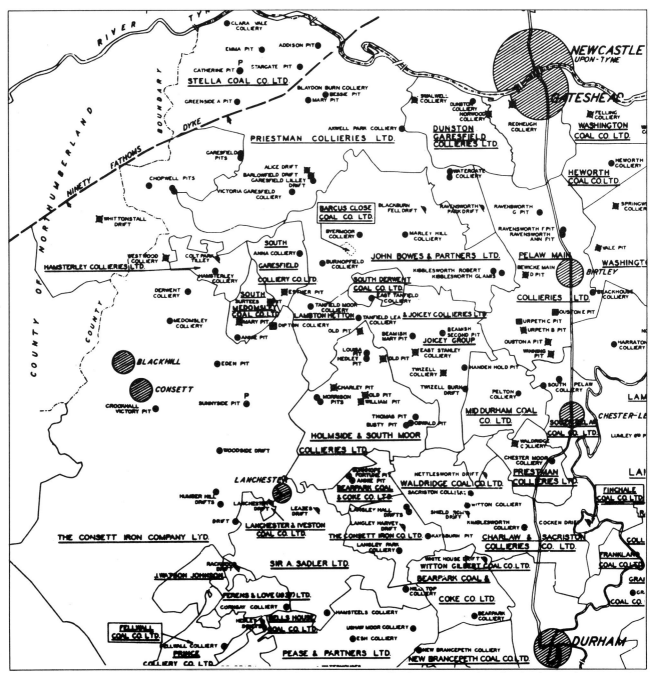

Map shownig coal companies and collieries prior to nationalisation in North-west Durham

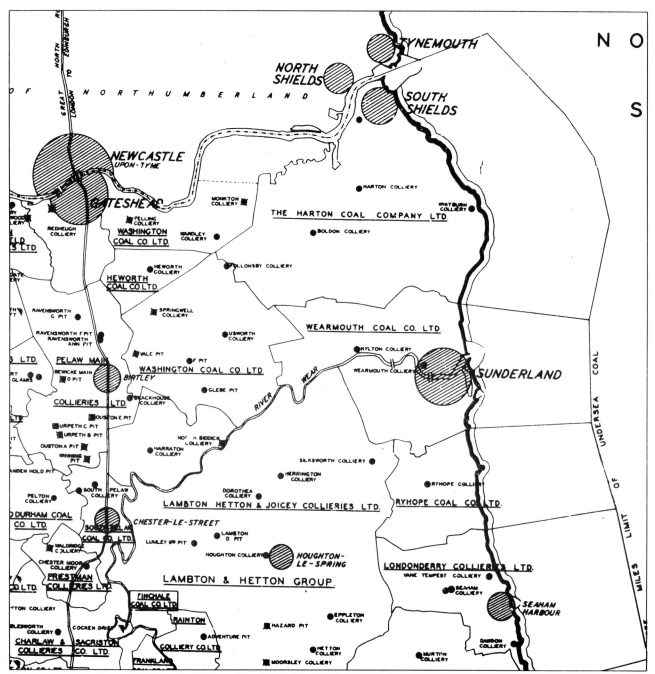

Map shownig coal companies and collieries prior to nationalisation in North-east Durham

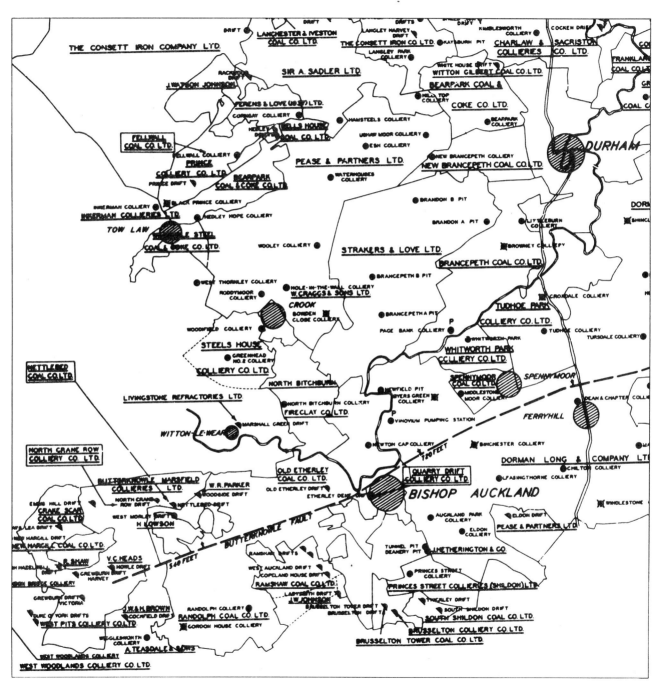

Map showing coal companies and collieries prior to nationalisation in South-west Durham

11

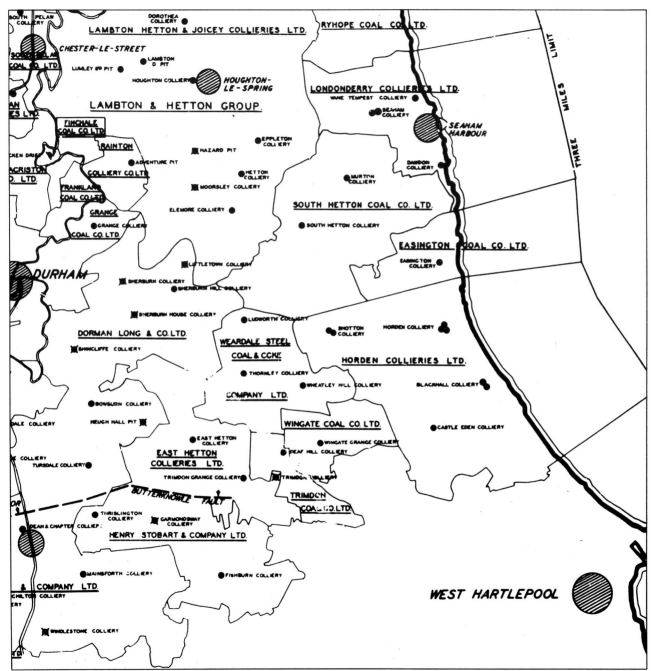

Map shownig coal companies and collieries prior to nationalisation in South-east Durham

No. 1 pit Chopwell colliery

CHOPWELL COLLIERY

The first record of coal mining in the Chopwell area is of Bell pits, leased from the Bishop of Durham, being worked in 1530, and there can be no doubt that the working of these shallow pits was extensive.

The first mention of a Chopwell colliery is an entry in 'Borings and Sinkings' which records that in 1795 the Maria pit had a shaft depth of 300ft to the Brockwell seam although the date of its sinking is earlier, believed to be 1756.

On August 22 1798 work began on the sinking of the Taylor pit to the 3/4 seam at a depth of 336ft, and before the turn of the century the North pit had been sunk to the Brockwell seam at 282ft. In 1802 the Penny Hill pit, also sunk to the Brockwell at 282ft, was added to this cluster of mines working in the Chopwell area.

Pits of this type and at this period in the development of mining technology would have a life expectancy of no more than 15 years, at which point they reached the limits of their ventilation and were abandoned in favour of a new sinking.

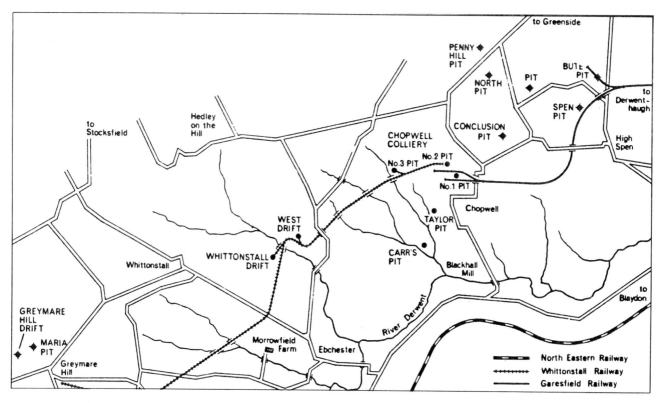

In 1864 the Consett Iron Company acquired the Chopwell royalty from the failed Derwent and Consett Iron Company and commissioned a series of borings which proved the existence of several seams of high quality coking coal in the area of Chopwell Woods. It was to extract these reserves that the company sank the No.1 pit at Chopwell colliery in May 1894. Almost immediately water and sand were encountered and progress was halted until an additt was driven from the shaft to the river Derwent at Blackhall Mill, through which the water was drained.

Within a year the No.2 pit was sunk to the Brockwell for the purpose of ventilation, but it was to be three years later in November 1897, that the first coals were raised from this seam. This new development made all those shafts that had hitherto been known as Chopwell colliery redundant.

For the small hamlet of Chopwell an era now began which was to transform the settlement into a bustling pit village destined to become one of the best known in Durham.

The turn of the twentieth century saw the company complete the building of a coke works alongside the No.1 pit, its massive crushing bunker dominating the skyline.

By 1906 the mine was electrified and a generating station was built which served the needs of the pit and the expanding colliery village. In the same year the No. 2 shaft was adapted for coal drawing.

The company's full royalty, The Chopwell and

Garesfield royalty, is confined by the river Derwent in the south-west, with the Ninety Fathom Dyke running down its north-west flank. The area is dissected by the Tantobie fault running north-south, which separates Garesfield colliery, sunk in the 18th century, from the Chopwell development. To the north the royalty crosses the county line into Northumberland, and it was to exploit these reserves that a drift mine was driven in 1907 to the Tilly seam.

The drift was driven at a spot two miles west of the colliery in the village of Whittonstall and was officially known as Whittonstall colliery, although local people called it Hardy's Drift.

From this new drift a narrow-gauge railway was laid to the screens at Chopwell. Two 56 HP, electrically powered narrow-gauge locomotives, each capable of pulling 250 tons of coal, served this rail link and were later, in 1909, joined by a third with a larger pulling capacity. Power was transmitted from the colliery power station to the locomotives by two overhead 500 volt cables and the locos were housed in sheds built at Chopwell. The line was further extended in 1908 when the West drift was sunk a quarter of a mile from Whittonstall.

In 1909 a third shaft, the No.3, was sunk, three quarters of a mile west of the No.1 pit to the Brockwell seam, replacing the No.2 as the main ventilation shaft for the colliery. This shaft also drew coals and rode men and materials and was served by an extension of the narrow-gauge railway.

A portent of things to come occurred in 1912 when the company sought to limit the hewer's earnings at Whittonstall colliery. The men responded by placing their own restriction on the number of tubs that they would collectively fill. One morning as the men-set was about to depart, a union official arrived and accused one of the

Photo: C. Downs.

No.1 pit from east c 1897. The coke ovens are under construction to right

No 3 pit headgear under construction 1909

Entrance to West drift 1908

hewers of filling more than his fair share of the quota they had imposed. The man in question refused to give way and sat tight in the set. So long as the recalcitrant hewer remained seated, the driver, Earnest Kidd, refused to take the set in-bye, and in a show of solidarity all the other miners alighted from the set. The dispute was only settled when the hewer agreed that he would not fill more tubs than the agreed amount again.

Sadly Earnest Kidd was killed in 1914 when a set of tubs from the No.3 pit ran out of control and collided with his locomotive.

The electric locomotives at Chopwell colliery were at the very frontier of electrical engineering technology and were far too often in the loco sheds being repaired. A particular weakness was the lubrication of the bearings, which could not cope with the strain of hauling the huge weight of coal and frequently overheated.

To relieve the pressure on the locos a main and tail hauler was installed next to the No.3 shaft, which became known as the Ravenside Hauler and pulled sets of 60 tubs, and the locos were demoted to pulling half sets up to the screens. This arrangement was to be short-lived. The electric locos had been a bold but disappointing experiment which was discontinued in 1923, when the Ravenside hauler was adapted to become the sole source of haulage power for the surface line.

The period from 1900 to the end of the First World

War marked the zenith of Durham's coal production, and the Chopwell complex's contribution was to produce three-quarters of a million tons of coal, employing 1,700 men. The coke works worked continuous at full capacity.

As in all areas where the coal seams outcrop, drifts are easily driven to exploit areas of coal isolated by faulted ground. Throughout the latter part of the 19th century and up to the 1950, a series of drifts was driven into the Hutton seam. These drifts, known as the Hutton drifts number perhaps as many as six in all.

The exact position of all of these drifts is uncertain but they made a substantial contribution to the production of Chopwell colliery.

The shortage of manpower created by the carnage of the First World War obliged the Consett Iron Company to close its Whittonstall drift and concentrate its manpower at Chopwell.

The rail link between the two undertakings was extended two miles to Greymare Hill to transport timber from the company's forest.

In 1917 the company re-entered some of the old workings in the area.

The first area re-entered was the 'Old Carrs pit', a drift driven by a Mr Carr in 1874, officially known as Milkwell colliery. This was entered through an underground connection from the No. 3 pit. Later the 'Old Taylors' pit of 1798 was re-entered. This colliery had once consisted of a drift

Photo: C. Downs

Electric locomotive on Whittonstall line c.1907

and a shaft. The shaft was reopened and a windlass installed, operated by two men.

By 1919 the Forest was exhausted and the rail link was removed, but this was the least significant event in a year that saw the full fury of Britain's working men burst into open revolt from London to the Clyde. This was the beginning of a decade that would make Chopwell one of the most famous of Durham's colliery villages, giving it the nickname Little Moscow.

Central to the development of the political tradition in Chopwell were several political families, epitomised by the Lawthers.

The Lawther brothers, Eddy, Herby, Andy Jack and Will, had made the journey from Choppington in Northumberland to settle in Chopwell in 1906. For two generations the family had been strongly influenced by the Primitive Methodist tradition and the grandfather had been an active Chartist. Their father and his brothers were strong trade unionists and active in the Co-operative movement. Will, the best known of the family was eventually to become the President of the Miners Federation of Great Britain.

In 1907 Will was elected Vice President of the Chopwell Lodge of the DMA. From 1908 to 1911 he was the Lodge delegate and by 1918 he had been elected to the Durham Executive.

In 1912 Will, like many of his contemporaries, took the opportunity of studying at the Central Labour Collage in London. While in London he met the Anarchist George Davidson, who had made a considerable amount of money by acquiring the sole rights to distribute Kodak film in Britain.

In 1913 George Davidson came to Chopwell and bought a shop in Derwent Street formally owned

Above: Looking towards Whittonstall drift 1908
Below: Trestle viaduct, 1908, later replaced by an
embankment **Photos: C. Downs**

Chopwell colliery No. 1 and No. 2 pit with crushing bunker for coke works, 1920

by Matt Caisley in which a political club was established which became the social focus for a number of men who were to play a major role in the events of the next two decades. They were men with anti-war inclinations, men who were either confirmed atheists, as was Vipond Millican Hardy, or men who were sceptical of the church's role in the affairs of working men

They formed a Socialist Sunday school, as a secular alternative for children and their parents, preaching socialist values.

During the first world war the club took an anti-war stand and Eddie Lawther was sentenced to two years hard labour for being a conscientious objector.

The patriotic fervour of the war years, kept the political club isolated from the rest of the village. But when the war was over and the village returned to the stark realities of post-war life the rebels from Matt Caisley's old shop in Derwent Street were at last to gain the ear of their fellow villagers. After all the sacrifice on the killing fields of France, a miner's life remained what it had been before; a constant struggle for survival. The disappointments of the post-war years, the looming economic crisis and the existence in the village of a politically educated group of men created an explosive social cocktail.

While the political club, or Communist club as it was known in the village, had its own library the influence of its members in the Miners Institute ensured that the Institute had itself an even more comprehensive library of books catering for a wide spectrum of interests, from the writings of Marx, Engels and Lenin to the great classics of English literature.

The leading socialists of the day were invited to

Chopwell miner's Welfare and Institute 1912

lecture at the institute and often addressed meetings packed to capacity.

T.A. Jackson, of the London Labour College, in his autobiography gives a graphic description of the series of lectures he gave in 1919:

'For the first lecture the hall was comfortably 'full' -that is, there were only a few vacant seats. For the second lecture it was quite full, and for the third it was crammed. And the audience swelled with each succeeding lecture until all the standing space was occupied and it became a real problem. Some slight relief was obtained when the colliers opened the windows and stood on the sills, leaning in over the top of the partly opened window-frame. The final lecture was given with the crowd all down the stairs, filling every gangway, and finally so crowding into the reading room at the back of the platform that, the front rank was leaning over the chairman (Will Lawther) and left me little more than six inches of space to stand in.'

The main parties represented in the village after 1921 were the Independent Labour Party and the Communist Party.

The balance of power between these groups can be gauged from the lodge banner unfurled in 1924.

The design of lodge banners in Durham was always the subject of much debate and discussion before a final design was agreed. The Chopwell banner of 1924 carried in equal prominence the insignia of both the Communist Party and the Labour Party alongside the portraits of Marx, Lenin and Keir Hardie. Marx was no doubt acceptable by both Labour Party and Communist Party members while Lenin represented the Communist Party and Keir Hardie the Labour Party. It would be a mistake to judge the relationship between the members of these parties by the criteria of today. The Russian revolution was only seven years old and had in 1917 been welcomed by hundreds of thousands of British workers. The leaders of the Chopwell lodge had developed together in an atmosphere of working-class self-education, they worked and lived together, they shared common aims and no doubt, in this decade at least, regarded the differences between them as slight compared with the enormous problems that they were collectively called upon to overcome.

There was a further and more unusual component to the Chopwell story and that was the role played by the colliery manager, Mr Imery. During the development of the library in the Chopwell Institute, Imery as colliery manager had taken the traditional position of the chairman of the Colliery Welfare Committee, effectively

Ravenside hauler

Outing at Blackhall Mill,1920

overseeing the affairs of the Institute. Furthermore he was regarded as an understanding and liberal man in his dealings with the miners. While this gained him some respect from the people of Chopwell it did not endear him to his employers, the Consett Iron Company. In 1925 when the company sought to impose new terms and conditions on the men, he was sacked and blamed for having allowed a militant lodge leadership to develop. It is said that he never recovered from this humiliation.

On March 26 1925 the miners of Chopwell colliery voted 1,100 to 286 to strike against the new terms demanded by the management. By May 3 1926, after 14 months of hardship, the Chopwell men remained defiantly on strike and were joined by the rest of the country in the General Strike.

That the Chopwell miners could last for so long on strike without yielding bears testimony to a high degree of village organisation. The Union had established a feeding centre and had underwritten the credit given to miner's families from the local shops, promising that if the credit advanced was not repaid by the men then the union would honour the debt. The two Co-operative stores in the village assisted with provisions, to be repaid after the strike in weekly payments. But what assisted the miners most was the progress that had been made by the Labour Party in gaining control of local government.

Blaydon District Council was controlled by Labour councillors who if not miners themselves were totally sympathetic to their cause. In the village they had already made their mark by naming three streets after Marx, his co-thinker Engles, and Lenin. But what was more valuable than their ability to name streets was their control of the Board of Guardians, the body responsible for the administration of relief to the poor. After increasing the scale of payments they made sure that no miner's family was refused assistance.

Of course the abundance of edible wild life in Chopwell's surrounding countryside and the miner's skill in catching the same, while remaining un-detected, was a not inconsiderable factor in the survival of the village.

As Chopwell entered its second year of struggle there is little evidence of resolve flagging. The colliery manager wrote to the Home Secretary complaining that the miners and their families in Chopwell were following the mine officials to the pit every morning humming the death march and singing other funeral hymns. The officials were intimidated to such an extent, he complained, that they were forced to returned to the practice of sleeping at the mine.

In May 1926, with the General Strike only days old, Chopwell Lodge was instrumental in making a call throughout the county for the organisation of Councils of Action, to unite communities together in the defence of the miners.

The Blaydon and Chopwell District Council of Action used the facilities at the disposal of its representatives on the Blaydon Urban District Council to produce a news sheet called The Northern Light. R.Page Arnot, the official historian of the Miners Federation of Great Britain, was to recall:

'H. Bolton, a local JP, Labour Leader and Chairman of the Boldon Urban District Council was reported to have gone to the U.D.C. offices on May 3, went round the numerous staff, instructed those he did not fully trust to take their holidays that first

Miners during 1926 lock-out digging for coal in Chopwell area

Work starts on the demolition of the coke bunker

fortnight in May - immediately - and turned the remaining staff, offices and machinery (including the duplicator) into an organ of the General Strike.'

The impact created by The Northern Light can be gauged by the how vigorously the authorities opposed its distribution. One miner was sentenced to prison for three months with hard labour. He was accused or committing an act ' likely to cause civil disaffection amongst the civil population' by distributing the journal.

Abandoned by the TUC after ten days the Chopwell community and the miners of Durham battled on for a further seven months and were forced to return to work in November. Even at the last ballot the county voted with a majority for continuing the strike for the first time but this failed to achieve the necessary two-thirds majority. It was December before the Chopwell men returned.

Despite the owner's promise that none would be victimised the revenge of the Consett Iron Company was undisguised.

The branch chairman Jack Gilland and all the Lawther brothers were refused work, as were Henry Bolton and Vipond Hardy and many others.

To compound the problems of the Lodge some 200 members broke away and joined the Non-Political-Union that had developed in the Nottinghamshire coalfield under the leadership of the M.P. George Spencer.

In Durham few miners had broken ranks and blacklegged, and the Non-Political Union was never a serious force. In general the owners never recognised its existence. However at Chopwell the owner negotiated a piece-rate agreement with the hewers of the Non-Political Union.

Two hewers who were members of the DMA sued the Consett Coal Company on the grounds that the Non-Political Union did not represent the majority of the men employed at the mine. They must have been more than surprised to win their case at the Newcastle County Court in these the darkest days for the trade union movement.

In the aftermath of the General Strike the mine itself was in bad shape and the No.2 pit was never to reopen. It stood idle and in 1931 its cages were removed. The No.1 and No.3 pit and the drift continued to work with a depleted workforce. Throughout the 1930s Chopwell's pit and community suffered the full effects of the great depression, until in 1939 the outbreak of war stimulated the demand for steel and therefore coking coal. But now many of the men who had sat on their hunkers throughout the depression were drafted into the Army and were no longer available for work at the mine. As in the First World War the drift was closed and production was concentrated at the Chopwell mine.

By 1946 the headgear at the No.2 pit was

Photo: D.G. Charlton

Garesfield incline 1956

Tubs in the sidings above West Drift, 1966

Photo: C.E. Mountford

The old No 2 pit engine house, now housing the Ravenside hauler 1966.

Photo: C.E. Mountford

26

dismantled and it was announced that the coke-works was to close. From now on Chopwell's coking coal was to be processed at the Derwenthaugh works near Dunston, on the outskirts of Gateshead.

The community of Chopwell must have been as pleased as any when in 1947 their aspirations were achieved when their pit was taken into nationalisation.

The post-war coal shortage breathed new life into Chopwell's flagging economy. By 1953 Whittonstall was reopened and another drift was driven to open up the three-quarter and the Brockwell seams, This drift was to be called the Child or Brockwell drift.

Now for the first time for more than two decades significant resources were at hand to upgrade Chopwell's aging infrastructure. The Ravenside hauler was relocated in the winderhouse of the redundant No.2 pit and the line was revitalised. The old No.2 pit screens were demolished and replaced by a new complex.

In 1955 the steam winder in the No.1 pit was replaced by a Robey Metropolitan Vickers electric winding engine. Underground the new administration had made some attempt to modernise the colliery, introducing plough faces and Huwood loaders in the Tilly seam, but in general the old methods - windy picks, cutters and explosives - persisted.

In 1957 the NCB separated the Whittonstall drifts from the Chopwell mine and operated them as separate units, provoking fears that perhaps one of these two operations did not have a long-term future.

In 1959 the wiring in the colliery houses was upgraded to the standard required by the new North Eastern Electricity Board. The old pit power station was now closed and Chopwell village was for the first time connected to the national grid. Fears for

Photo: C.E. Mountford

No. 1 pit after closure

27

the long-term future of the Chopwell mine were further aroused when in the same year recruitment of labour at the colliery ceased.

In 1960 coal drawing at the No.3 pit ceased. It was not however all bad news as a new drift was to be driven close to the old West drift of 1908, which was reopened as a ventilation drift for the new workings. A 200 HP electric motor was installed at the drift entrance to haul the tubs up the 500 yards, one-in-eight incline to the surface. The new drift was opened on August 22 1960, and four days later the Union was informed that the No.1 shaft would no longer be drawing coal and all production would be concentrated on the drifts.

In 1961 the No.2 shaft was filled and capped, the Garesfield railway was dismantled and all coal and materials were transported by road. During the course of 1963 all the surface buildings were demolished at the No.3 pit and the shaft was capped in 1964. In the same year the last of Chopwell's shafts, the No.1 pit, was filled and capped, but the heapstead and winding engine remained until 1966 when they were dismantled and removed.

The famous Chopwell banner

The Whittonstall, East and West drifts did not survive 1966, they were closed, and what men still wanted to remain in the industry were transferred to other collieries, some making the long journey each day to Westoe colliery, South Shields and Wearmouth colliery, Sunderland.

28

Photo: Alan Kennedy   *Cutting the first sod Dawdon colliery 1899*

DAWDON COLLIERY

The decision by the sixth Marquess of Londonderry to sink Dawdon colliery was in response to problems which were being encountered at his Seaham colliery.

As Seaham Colliery's workings pushed out to the south-east it became increasingly costly to work these reserves from the old pit's shafts. The decision was therefore made to sink new shafts at a rocky promontory known as Noses Point by the edge of the chilly waters of the North Sea. Close

On August 26 1899 the first sod of the first shaft was cut by Theresa Marchioness of Londonderry and her son Lord Castlereagh was to cut the first sod of the second shaft, the two shafts being christened the Theresa and the Castlereagh respectively.

Almost immediately the sinking encountered the same difficulties that had dogged the sinking of the nearby Murton colliery some 60 years earlier. Once having penetrated the layer of sand beneath the limestone the shafts were engulfed in water which fed into the shaft at a rate of 7,000 gallons per minute, far too much for the pumping system to manage.

The Dawdon sinkers and their employers, however, were destined to avoid the long and debilitating struggle with the waters of the sand feeder that drove Colonel Braddyll, Murton's founder, to the bankruptcy courts. The mining engineers at the end of the 19th century had a brand new weapon in their armoury in the form of the Poetsch freezing method. Dawdon Colliery was only the second colliery in the County of Durham to freeze a shaft in order to overcome the problem of water. The first was at Washington earlier in the same year.

by was the ancient settlement of Dawdon, formerly Daldwin or Dalden which had changed little in the preceding centuries.

Daldon Tower was built soon after the Norman conquest and was the home of the Lords of Dalden, who ruled that region for many centuries. Dalton Towers became the favoured seat of the Bower family, ancestors of the present British monarch.

On May 16 1902 the Theresa shaft had reached a depth of 350ft, and was almost through the limestone when its progress was halted to allow the sinkers in the Castlereagh shaft to catch up. On April 20 1903 both shafts were through the limestone and the sinking operation was handed over to the German company of Gebhart and Koenig of Northaven.

A series of bore holes, 28 in all at each pit, was drilled at equal distances around a circle 30ft in diameter. Each bore hole was drilled to a depth of 484ft, tapering from a diameter of ten inches at the surface to six inches at the bottom. After these boreholes had been lined with steel tubes, second tubes were inserted, down which a cooling agent, a mixture of brine, chloride of magnesia and ammonia, was passed returning to bank via the gap between the inner tube and the walls of the bore hole. At the surface a bank of compressors cooled the liquid before recycling it back through the tubes.

Before the sinkers could take advantage of this new and revolutionary method a further obstacle had to be surmounted. It was found that the water in the two shafts rose and fell in unison with the tide, due to the close proximity of the shafts to the sea. This was having the effect of slowing down the cooling process, and to overcome this problem the shaft bottoms had to be sealed with cement above the depth of the water feeders. After all the efforts to excavate the shafts they now had to be backfilled with cement.

The engineer in charge of the sinking, Mr. Wood,

Sinking operations Dawdon colliery c 1900

31

noted in his diary:

Erection of Castlereagh heapstead

'From July 20th to 22nd 1904 one hundred and ninty tons of concrete were put down the Castlereagh shaft, filling the bottom crib of tubbing, and this stopped the water flow.'

Slowly a wall of ice formed around the shaft, solidifying the dangerous alliance of sand and water. Now the sinkers proceeded, blasting their way through the frozen mass and lining the shaft with cast iron sections as they proceeded. The sinkers had to proceed with extreme caution. The amount of explosives used was critical, as a miscalculation could expose the cooling tubes and even breach the ice wall, causing a fatal inrush of water into the shaft.

Despite the best efforts of the sinkers the shafts were not completed without tragedy. On September 6 1907, just one month before the sinking was complete, Henry Dunn and George Attwood were killed when a huge power cable crashed down the Castlereagh shaft. The men had been slowly descending in a kibble. Their descent was illuminated by an electric light that was powered from the surface generator through a long and heavy cable. They had nearly reached the bottom of the shaft when a sharp crack was heard and the entire length of cable plunged down the shaft. Its vast weight and the incredible velocity of its descent gave little chance of survival for the unfortunate men below. While the community was still reeling from this

tragedy, and within the short space of a week, fate struck again when a cradle collapsed in the same shaft, killing three men; Thomas Brown(25), his brother George Brown(23), and Robert Briggs(30).

These men had all been working some distance down the shaft when the chains from which their cradle was suspended gave way on one side. The unfortunate men plunged 200ft to their deaths.

Dawdon colliery ambulance team, 1913
Standing from left to right: J, Turnbull, G. H. Doxford, W. G. Pigg (Capt.), J. Burt
Sitting from left to right: Dr. F. W. Squair (Instructor), J. Robinson, W. Barry, T. H. Lloyd (Hon. Sec.)

Photo: Easington District Council

The death of the two Brown brothers was particularly sad as their father, a master mason at the colliery, had died only two months earlier, widowing their mother. The brothers were the sole means of support for her and her younger family. Both brothers had been coffin bearers for Henry Dunn, one of the victims of the first accident. That so much misery could be inflicted on one family in so short a period of time was sadly by no means uncommon in mining communities.

The sinking of Dawdon colliery was officially concluded on October 5 1907. Now, with the community still mourning the tragic events of September, Dawdon began its remarkably productive life.

Simultaneously the Hutton, Harvey, Low Main and Five Quarter were developed. Districts previously being worked by Seaham colliery were now worked from Dawdon's shafts by men transferred from Seaham.

Dawdon village, once a hamlet of 83 houses, was extended by Londonderry, who built 20 streets of new housing to accommodate the rapidly rising workforce. By 1910 3,300 miners were producing one million tons of hand-hewed coal per year. In the traditions of lordly paternalism Londonderry built a church to cater for the spiritual needs of the miners and their families, while the miners, by deductions from their wages, built a recreation park and a sports ground at Dawdon Dene.

At the time of the sinking the workforce was represented by the Seaham Colliery Lodge of the DMA. But after production began the men required their own checkweighman. The post was advertised and finally, after a selection process, filled by Dick Lawson in March 1908. Four months after being voted Checkweighman Dick was made Dawdon's first lodge secretary, a position he was to hold until 1942.

Dick Lawson was born at Whitehaven in Cumberland in 1874 , the eldest son of a family of 12. His brother Jack was to become the MP for Chesterfield and later Lord Lawson of Beamish. Dick started work in the pit at Whitehaven at the age of 12, working for a shilling (5p) a day. In 1891 the whole family moved to Boldon colliery where Dick worked before moving to Hylton colliery and then to Dawdon.

Dick's interests were not confined solely to the union as he was elected to the District Council in 1912 as one of the first Labour members.

Under the stewardship of Dick the lodge developed a reputation for militancy which raised the rates of pay of the Dawdon miners substantially above the county average.

Prior to 1926 conditions in the Durham coalfield were substantially better than in other coalfields. Since 1880 the working hours for hewers, by far the most numerous section of the workforce, were reduced to between 6 and 6 1/2 hours, depending on the colliery. It is no wonder then that the coal-owner's plans to introduce a universal eight hour shift were so strongly opposed in the Durham coalfield. If Durham miners in general were more united and were the last to return to work in 1926 it was almost entirely due to the fact that they had the most to lose of any group of miners. Dawdon miners were no exception.

On November 30 1926 the Durham agents signed an agreement with the county Coal Owners Association increasing the working day for hewers to 7 1/2 hours and to 8 hours for all other classes of workmen. Wages were to be reduced by an average of 21 per cent. This agreement was never endorsed by the rank-and-file miners who by a majority of 8,000 votes rejected the document. It was only the fact that the majority failed to reach 65 per cent of the votes cast that secured a return to work.

It is not difficult to imagine Durham miners' state of morale as they lifted their tokens to resume work after seven months sacrifice, returning under an agreement that gave substantially worse conditions than had been in force at the time the dispute had started.

In the years that were to follow it was the view of the Durham-based leadership that after such a defeat further resistance to the owners was to be avoided. In 1929 the miners of Dawdon were to offer another view in a struggle that stands as one of the most remarkable in the history of the coalfield

To understand the Dawdon lockout of 1929, it is necessary to know something of the conditions prevailing in the coalfield in the preceding three years.

The concluding agreement of the November 30, 1926 was by no means the end of the attack on the miners' wages and conditions. This agreement specified that it could be concluded within one month by either side, and in the September of 1927 the employers yet again moved to reduce wage rates across the county, using the excuse that the cost-of-living index had fallen.

Because of failure to secure the agreement of the union the matter was settled by Sir William Plenner, the 'independent' chairman of the district wages board.

The resultant judgement became known as the Plenner Award and granted the owners a reduction of the minimum wage from 6s 8½d to 6s 1d and the minimum addition to basic rates to be reduced from 89 per cent to 65 per cent, a general reduction in wages that reduced miners' wages to their pre-First World War level.

The wounds of '26 were now smarting with new salt, to the extent that in the weeks after March 1, 1928, the date the Plenner award was implemented, a wave of strikes and restrictions swept through the coalfield. These actions were bitter, but short-lived.

The miners' union at pit level was suffering attacks on all fronts. In the same year the Government passed the Trades Disputes and Trade Union Act 1927, severely curtailing the ability of unions to pursue trade disputes and outlawing sympathy actions. This act, however, was not the only factor that was inhibiting union resistance. The slackness in trade, a precursor of the great depression of the 30s, had resulted in 50,000 of

Dawdon lock-out 1929

the county's 150,000 miners being made unemployed. The fear of unemployment was a powerful damper on militancy.

Then there was the threat posed by non union members and members of the break-away union. Although Durham had remained more solid than any other in 1926 a small percentage of miners had broken away and returned to work. An attempt was made in the year after the end of the strike to organise these men into the Non-Political Union of George Spencer which predominated in the Nottinghamshire Coalfield.

Lord Castlereagh, the heir to the Londonderry title, even tried to establish a branch of the Industrial Peace Union that had been set up by J.A. Seddon, a former president of the TUC, and Havelock Wilson, the notorious right-wing leader of the seamen's union. He appeared not to have met with much success.

On the left a new force was developing in the coalfield. This was the industrial arm of the British Communist Party in the form of the Minority Movement (MM). During the 1926 strike the policy of the Communist Party, directed from Moscow, was to call upon the miners to put all their faith in the General Council of the TUC. They particularly wanted to maintain the support that the left-wing members of the General Council were giving to the Anglo-Russian Trade Union Committee.

After the TUC sold out in 1926 and in response to internal problems in the Soviet Union the international Communist movement under the leadership of Stalin made a sharp lurch to the left, condemning all leaders of the union movement as potential traitors and characterising the Social Democratic and Labour parties throughout Europe as 'social fascists'.

This policy was to have disastrous consequences in Germany but also influenced events in Dawdon in 1929.

During the course of the wage reductions the Minority Movement had agitated for a harder line from the officials in Durham and for a county strike ballot. It is difficult to asses the exact strength of the MM in the coalfield, but it is known that about 30 Lodges were supporting this policy.

By January 1929 the Dawdon Lodge was weathering the storm better that most. The strength of the Lodge in the past had won agreements that protected their wages from the affects of the bad geological conditions which were from time to time encountered in the mine. One such agreement was the hitch agreement that protected earnings if the coal seam was to move vertically more than so many inches.

Jakie Hall was 16 at the time and some 60 years latter he was to recall:

'There was still a lot of antagonism between some of the management after the '26 strike. It wasn't always obvious but you could tell by the way they talked. The '29 strike had to do with the "inch agreement". If you were hewing in a place where you had an up or downward fault it had to be at least six inches before you got paid. The men were unhappy about that.

Then they [the management] tried time without number to reduce the percentage. Doing piece work you had to fill so many tubs before you got the mini [minimum wage], which was four shillings and sixpence [per shift][23pence] before you got your 65 per cent on top.

I was cleaning out the hard coal cutting machine at the time of the strike, they called it "scraping out". That was about the hardest job I did, you used some sweat no doubt about it, but with the percentage it was a canny wage for a lad. Of course the cutter made sure you worked hard because his wages were involved as well. See the only trouble with the percentage was that if you were working in bad conditions you spent a lot of time trying to keep yourself safe, and if the coal was hard you couldn't fill as many tubs and you were stuck with the mini'.

On January 8 1929 Malcolm Dillon, Londonderry's agent, sent a letter Frederick Wilson, manager of Dawdon Colliery, stating:

'The time has come when it is imperative that the Dawdon costs should be reduced and brought nearer to the county average and practice. This particularly applies to the cost in connection with the hitches which have been very onerous to the colliery for a long period.

I shall be glad if you will take this matter up with the men with a view to obtaining a reduction in costs and putting Dawdon colliery on the same footing as other collieries.'

A meeting between the manager and the men took place, where the manager outlined his proposals for new agreements covering the special payments, but on February 4 Lawson wrote to Wilson informing him that the men had deferred any decision until the 24th of the month.

The lodge was obviously playing for time and the manager knew it. He responded two days later:

'Unless you are prepared to meet me, on or before Monday the 11th instant, the offer made to you will be withdrawn and other necessary steps will be taken to effect essential reductions.'

Up to this point Lawson had made no attempt to get in touch with the Durham Agents, who had in the past advocated a non-confrontational line, seeking to agree on reductions rather than oppose them by industrial action.

The Dawdon Lodge, however, appeared unruffled by this threat and stood fast to the Lodge's decision to wait until the 24th.

Equally intransigent were Londonderry's agents, who on February 15 issued notices to the Dawdon miners of his intention to lock the men out, to take effect on March 2. In the letter sent to Henry Armstrong, Londonderry's representative to the Durham Coal Owners Association, the agents hope that:

'It is probable that the Durham Agents will now take the matter in hand and I am of the opinion that we should ask that piece workers be reduced to say 25 per cent above the county average. Houses in turn should be abolished [the practice of issuing colliery houses on a rota basis]. Starting to put and hew in turn should be abolished. Cavils should be put in every six months instead of every 12 weeks as at present.

I shall be obliged for your view and instructions on this matter'.

In his reply Armstrong showed some concern that the issues were going further than was first intended but expressed optimism that the Durham Agents would soon be involved.

It seems certain from these exchanges that the issuing of notices was a deliberate tactic to take the matter out of the 'militant' Dawdon miners' hands and into those of the more reasonable Durham Agents.

If this were the case then they had made a misjudgement, as by the time the notices were due to take effect the Durham Agents had not been contacted by the Dawdon Lodge and therefore they in turn had not contacted Londonderry's representatives. Nor had the Lodge made any attempt to negotiate with Wilson. Subsequently on March 2 1929 3,800 miners at Dawdon colliery were locked out.

Although Lawson had not contacted the Dawdon manager he had sought a meeting with Londonderry himself on March 3, and the lodge resolved that they would neither work nor hold a meeting until Londonderry agreed to meet their delegation. However, on March 7 the lodge did meet Wilson to discuss the reductions but were unable to reach agreement.

Again Jakie Hall recalls:

'The meetings at the miners' Hall in Dawdon were always packed to the balcony, you couldn't get in. I was only a lad at the time so I wasn't actively involved, but you could tell they [the miners] were confident'.

On Sunday March 10 the Lodge had a further meeting and on this occasion agreed to contact their Durham headquarters and seek the intervention of the Durham agents. Consequently W.P.Richardson, agent for the DMA, met the manager Wilson, upon which he was offered new terms of employment for the Dawdon men. These new terms were not as draconian as those first suggested by Wilson and were recommended to the Lodge by the Durham leadership. A ballot was held of the Dawdon men between March 18 and 21 which rejected the offer with 752 votes for and 1,052 against. Both management and union leaders had been firmly rebuffed and the scene was set for a direct confrontation, the backdrop of which was a General Election campaign.

At this time the majority of Dawdon's men were represented in Parliament by Sydney Webb, the well known Fabian. Webb had decided not to stand for a further term of office, and was to be replaced by Ramsay MacDonald, the leader of the Labour Party in the spring election of 1929. What the local miners did not know at the time was that this champion of the cause of Labour was also a firm personal friend of the noble Lord Londonderry and was in the habit of exchanging intimate letters with his wife.

The fact that the leader of the Labour Party was standing in Seaham attracted the attention of the Secretary of the Communist Party of Great Britain, the accomplished orator Harry Pollitt. Pollitt stood in the election as the Communist candidate for Seaham.

When the Dawdon lockout materialised it must have appeared, to the Communist Party a confirmation of the validity of their new line. Here at Dawdon colliery were workers in a struggle not just against their employers but against an area leadership which was advocating a compromise on the employer's terms.

In an attempt to persuade the men to reverse their decision the lodge officials, who were now supporting the stand of the area leadership, organised a second ballot. Before the ballot they organised a meeting to which the DMA Executive Committee had been invited, while the Communist Party held their own meetings urging the men not to weaken.

The result of the second ballot was an increased majority in favour of rejecting the owner's terms. On this occasion 1,159 were for rejection and 735 for acceptance.

By the third week of the dispute Londonderry was sufficiently concerned to change his original decision not to become directly involved, and he agreed to meet the area officials of the DMA. At this meeting further concessions were made to the union. Londonderry proposed that if the men would accept the piece rate reductions the questions of special payments for hitches and other faults could go to arbitration.

The DMA regarded these terms as the best that had been achieved for any lodge in the county but on April 19 a third ballot of the Dawdon men resulted in a greater margin than ever between those in favour of continuing the dispute and those willing to accept the company's terms. On this occasion 1,221 were for rejection while 727 were for acceptance.

By this time it was obvious that the Communist Party was gaining influence and recruits among the Dawdon miners. They were organising meetings and issued a strike bulletin advocating the election of a new strike committee, excluding all those opposed to the strike. They also called for the extension of the strike to all the Seaham collieries and the organisation of communal feeding. It was to be in the execution of this last demand that the Communist Party was to be most successful.

International Workers Aid was an organisation set up by the Communist International to provide solidarity in the form of food to workers involved in industrial action and to ensure, as far as possible, that trade unionists should not be starved back to work. Ancrum, a Communist councillor from Felling, Gateshead, was dispatched to Seaham with £30 from this organisation to set up a kitchen to provide meals for the families of the Dawdon miners. Initially they were met with the combined resistance of both management and union, who

James Ancrum addressing miners at Dawdon colliery, 1929

attempted to prevent them hiring a suitable hall. By June, however. The kitchen was established in the Co-operative Hall and provided considerable quantities of hot meals for the Dawdon miners and their families.

Dawdon families were sufficiently impressed with the Communist Party for 2,000 to attend a May Day demonstration in Dawdon addressed by Harry Pollitt and James Ancrum.

The stubborn refusal of the Dawdon miners to bend to the mineowners' demands so soon after the defeat of '26 is remarkable. However fresh forces were to enter the scene to effect a solution. J. Ramsay MacDonald, now the Prime Minister of the new Labour government, was asked by the lodge to intervene and appoint an intermediary in an attempt to break the dead lock.

W.L.Cook of the Government's Mines Department was duly appointed and negotiated a return to work on the basis of the offer given to the Durham agents on the 18th of July, with the proviso that the outstanding question of the payments while working in faulted ground should be settled by arbitration if no agreement was reached by June 29.

In order to avoid rejection by yet a fourth ballot the issue was settled this time by a show of hands, and it was agreed to return to work on July 13 and to put the outstanding issues to arbitration.

The dispute was however by no means over. A true measure of the degree of disillusionment the miners now had in their own lodge officials was demonstrated when they elected three men to represent them at arbitration. The men rejected their own officials and elected A.J.Cook, Secretary of the MFGB, Harry Pollitt, the leader of the Communist Party and George Lumley, the communist checkweighman at Ryhope colliery. In the event it was Lumley, who had come second in the election, who represented the Lodge.

It is clear that Lumley's tactic, and by implication the tactic of the Communist Party, was to refuse to accept any agreement which worsened

Workers International Relief and Dawdon miners 1929

the conditions of the Dawdon miners.

Lumley's prolonged prevarications exasperated all parties with the exception of the Dawdon rank and file, who consistently supported him and accepted his guidance, rejecting the advice of their own lodge officials.

By August 8th in a letter to J.M.Blackwell, one of the Durham officials, Ramsay MacDonald expresses his frustration:

'I cannot conceal from you my quiet concern about the way that your affairs are being handled by a communist of the type of Lumley. Lumley can no more settle a dispute than my boot can, nor has he any intention of doing so....

Can you do nothing to clear Lumley out on account of his incompetence? If you would face him up to the hard facts of failure to do anything, things would begin to get done'.

By late September 1929 neither had Lumley agreed to any solution nor had he agreed to the appointment of an umpire other than Dr.Dunstan, another local Communist and therefore totally unacceptable to the other side.

Again the Mines Department intervened, offering to break the deadlock by itself appointing an umpire. A lodge meeting held on September 29 again rejected the advice of both the DMA and lodge officials and voted to allow Lumley to address the lodge. By the end of the meeting they had decided to let the letter from the Mines Department 'Lie on the table', a well-known trade union euphemism for a back-heel.

The exasperated owners decided on October 3 to return to the tactics of confrontation and announced that they had no alternative but to close the colliery. They deferred the decision for one week and it was now time for the officials of the DMA to play their trump card.

Now threatened with a second lock-out within three months the men were told the harsh facts of life : If there was to be a second dispute then the DMA would provide no strike pay. Only on this basis and under this degree of pressure did the Dawdon men agree to the Inspector of Mines' proposals for the appointment of an independent umpire.

November 4 saw the end to the dispute when Department of Mines appointee Sir Harrold Morris KC opted for the solution that had been offered by the owners on July 12.

Just two days later, on Wednesday November 6, just before midnight five miners were working at the coal face in the Low Main seam of the Castlereagh pit when a huge quantity of heavy post sandstone fell from the roof, cutting them off from the out-bye roadway.

Rescuers frantically tunnelled under the stone to reach the trapped men. After hours of strenuous labour communication was established between three of the victims, and by 9.00am the passage to these men was sufficiently large to drag them to safety relatively unharmed. By noon of the same

day the two missing men were located but they were dead, crushed by the fall.

The rescued men were Thomas Meek (35), Thomas Hope (25), and James Morgan (20). William Charles Emery (25) and John Phelan (19) perished.

With this tragedy dominating the life of the community the year of 1929 drew to a close and Dawdon entered the era of the great depression of the 1930s. For over a decade the colliery was to suffer from lay-offs and short-time working.

In 1932 1,800 men were paid off.

In 1933 the whole colliery was laid off when a fire at the Theresa shaft destroyed much of the heapstead.

By the end of the decade and even after the declaration of war the lay-offs continued. 700 were paid off as late as 1940, and in an effort to minimise the extent of the hardship the Lodge operated a rota system where everyone worked two weeks out of three, taking it in turns to spend a week on the dole.

It was the demands of the war effort and the post-war coal shortage that finally restored Dawdon colliery to its former glory.

Dawdon in the 1950's was a massive coal-producing machine. Production methods had changed very little over the years due to the relatively good geological conditions. The introduction of windy picks in some parts of the mine and belt conveyers on long wall faces appear to be the extent of changes made in over 40 years. All the hewers and putters were on piece earnings and each flat had its own payments particular to the prevailing conditions. The miners' lodge at the colliery was in a constant state of protracted negotiations with the management over prices. In addition to the central role of wage bargaining the miners lodge had to be represented at Durham,

Salaries the Same.

	W McCloud	15
Chairman }	R. Bell	1063
	B. Lawson	630

Treasurer   Jas. Shaw   R
Secretary   Sam. Barratt   R
Ass. Treas.   G. Holmes   R
"   Sec   Jim Lewlin   R
Compensation Sec.   T. Hope   R
Delegate   Enn. Lambert   R

Auditor   R. HEDLEY   T. LAMB

Unemployment Sec.   Jno Shaw   R
Labour Party Del.   W Spence   R
Institute Sec.   R Woodhouse   R
R. Aimers Sec.   T Littlefair   R
Band Chairman   W Spence   R
Band Treasurer   A Whittington   R

Brakemen.
R. McBeth   R
. Kinty   R
G. Maxted   R
. McCloud   R

Housing Committee

S. Barratt
R. Bell

Card Markers.

Wit Beardmore	516	905
T Bremner Jun	569	910
Gordon Carr	533	852
Law Duffy	296	
Tom Gilbech	290	
G Goodridge	514	942
Jno W Howe	143	
Geo Jeffries	273	
T.W. Kidley	211	
Law McAvennie	118	
Jas McLoran	179	

Average Takers.

Matt Bell	1151
Wm Carr	932
Jno Hall	554
Alx Williams	946

Pit Inspectors

G Campbell	881
Tom Fenwick	1041
Jos Foots	319
R Hedley	630
Ed Morris	569
A Whittington	290

provide a service to its unemployed members, look after the retired members, regulate the allocation of colliery houses, inspect the pit, administer the Welfare Hall and, not least, fight the compensation cases when men were unfortunately injured at work. The lodge was not so much a branch of a union as a form of local government.

Fortunately at Dawdon the agreements book, a form of lodge diary of events, covering the period of the 50's has survived. It makes fascinating reading. Between the hand-written National, Area, and Local agreements are short notes describing mishaps, accidents and deaths.

An entry dated 26/7/51 states:

'A breakage occurred in the Castlereagh shaft on Thursday morning, 7.20am on the 26/7/51. A tub of coal and a tub of stone went down the shaft, from the height of the Low Main level. The Thursday night shift (Castlereagh side) were laid idle. On Friday the three shifts were laid idle but normal work was resumed on Monday morning 30/7/51

The damage to the shaft was 12 broken skeets and stringers. The balance rope was also damaged and a new one was put on. The cause of the accident is as yet unknown but it is believed that the tubs jumped the controller.'

Six months later a more serious shaft accident is recorded:

'The first cage of hewers which descended in fore shift on 31/1/52 went too fast for some reason yet to be defined and crashed into the crossing baulks at the Low Main level Theresa shaft.

'There were 43 men in the cage and all were more or less injured. Thirty eight reported accidents or shock and one or two who went in-bye to work had to come out again.

Besides shock other injuries were four fractured legs and one dislocation.'

Six weeks later a short but sad entry informs us that:

'A fatal accident occurred in the South East drift on the above date [19/3/52] when J.

Photo: Alan Kennedy

Hewing in a development place, Main Coal Dawdon colliery 1950s

Poney putting in development, Dawdon colliery 1959

Bolton, a puller aged 49, residing at 53 Ash Crescent was killed by a fall of stone.

'A first pull was being made from a new advancing face in 18 South district, South East drift, Low Main seam. The puller Pat Bolton was busy drawing brattice timber when a stone 5'x3' by 12" thick fell upon him.

It was thought that he was killed instantly though he was not certified dead until the doctor examined him. He leaves a widow and family. Boy(15) stepson, girl(20) stepdaughter and married daughter.'

Fatal accidents through falls of stone accounted for the vast majority of accidents at a time when the roof was supported almost exclusively by timber.

An entry made one year later reads:

A Maudlin hewer working in 12 West South Maudlin was fatally injured by a fall of stone at approx. 7.00 pm on Monday 28/6/54.

'He was working with his marrow Tom Lamb when a slip came away from the roof and he was badly injured. He died on the road out-bye.

The night shift in the Theresa pit was loosed out but the stone men and the shooters descended at their usual time 10.00pm. The deceased got to bank about 9.15pm.

'Bank hands were given a break at 9.30.'

This entry illustrates how after nationalisation the tradition of mineworkers to lay the whole pit idle (loose the pit) for a full day after a fatal injury was modified by agreement with the management, It was generally agreed locally that any man in the shift and the district where the fatality occurred was allowed to go home and be paid but other shifts that day would be expected to work. At Dawdon it was agreed with the management that the bank hands would be given a break after a fatal injury rather than go home and lose a whole shift.

While the majority of deaths occurred at Dawdon underground and on the face this was not exclusively the case.

On November 25 1955 an explosion occurred opposite the ambulance station killing Alfred Raymond Snaith, a run rider aged 31, and badly injuring Robert J Patterson, a hewer.

A fire had been started to burn rubbish, amongst which had been placed two metal pipes which were filled with concrete. These pipes had been used as supports during the war when timber was in short supply. The report states that there must have been an air pocket in the pipes which caused the concrete to be ejected out of the pipe at one end with such force that the pipe was flung towards the two men, with fatal consequences.

Throughout the 50's the average earnings of the Dawdon men steadily increased to a level that would have astounded the men of 1929. In 1956 at the bottom of the piece workers' earnings league were the putters, who averaged 55 shillings and six pence a shift, £13.00 per week, and at the top were the pullers, who were compensated for this

the most dangerous work of the three shift cycle by a massive 101 shillings and threepence a shift, £25 per week. Considering that the going rate for manual workers in other industries was in the region of £6.00 a week Dawdon's reputation as a high-paying pit was well-earned.

The militancy of the piece work men and an example of how they were constantly squeezing

Stonemen Charley Gierson (right), Bob Bell (left) preparing new access road to skip shaft

new payments out of the management can be seen from this entry in the agreements book for March 1957.

'Middle Main Pullers Payment for tripper:

'Owing to a depression or swally in the Middle Main Coal face the belt in the depression had to be lifted by means of a tripper that levelled the belt over the depression.

The pullers claimed for additional payment for the extra work involved. After protracted negotiations it was agreed that the price be fixed at 5/- [Five shillings-25p] base on 12/6 [12 shillings and six pence 60p] gross per pull.

The lodge had asked for 7/6 [seven shillings and six pence-39p] base per pull'.

On November 24 1959 the management announced that due to the high ash content of the coal that was being mined in the 7th west district of the Main Coal they were closing the district and deploying the men to other districts.

Mercifully Dawdon escaped a large disaster. However, had it not been for the cool head of Peter Parkinson on the last day of 1959 many men could have lost their lives.

The men were transported in-bye by a men-set known as Paddy's Mail. Because it was New Year's Eve the night shift men had been moved forward six hours and descended the mine at 9.35 am. The set was standing at the out-bye landing and after a number of men had boarded the set it started to run down an incline, totally out of control. As it gained momentum one miner broke his leg jumping from the set. Peter Parkinson however worked his way towards the front tram where he applied the brake bringing the set to rest. Most of the men returned to bank in a state of

Theresa headgear and timberyard ramp

shock where they were treated in the ambulance station. Peter's name was forwarded to the Daily Herald by his grateful workmates and he received their award for bravery on Saturday April 30.

1959 was the end of an era at Dawdon colliery. Winning coal solely by muscular strength was to become a thing of the past as mining entered the age of the power-loader. A change to these

Photo: Alan Kennedy

Timberyard and empty sidings

methods was essential if Dawdon was to exploit the huge reserves that lay to the east under the North Sea.

It had been planned to reconstruct the colliery, raising the output of coal from 700,000 tons a year to 900,000 tons, with a reduced number of men.

Central to this reorganisation was the replacement of the Castlereagh and the Theresa steam winders with two modern, tower-mounted, electrically powered friction winders.

The new winding system installed at Dawdon consisted of two cages running side by side in the shaft, connected together by four suspension ropes fastened to the roofs of both cages and passing over the main driving pulleys of the friction

Low Main level shaft kip 1958

Photo: Alan Kennedy

Surface heapstead No. 5 inspection belt 1958

Photo: Alan Kennedy

Castlereagh shaft bottom, west side.

Photo: Alan Kennedy

Castlereagh shaft surface 1959

Reconstruction work 1959

winder, which was mounted directly above the shaft in a tower. The underside of each cage was connected by a rope balance wheel equal in weight to that of the four ropes connecting the tops of the cages.

The advantage of this system is that a main driving pulley mounted directly above the shaft requires less energy than one mounted to the side. The disadvantage is that the power is transmitted from the motor to the ropes by the friction between the rope and the linings of the pulley wheel. This puts a limit on how fast the cages can be accelerated or retarded before the rope slips on the pulley wheels.

The Theresa shaft was fitted with a 2,000 h.p.d.c.

motor while the Castlereagh was fitted with a 1,000 h.p.d.c. motor.

By July 18 1960 the modernisation was sufficiently advanced for the colliery to change over to skip winding, but not without problems, as this entry in the lodge diary shows:

'Dawdon colliery changed over to skip winding. There was a lot of trouble with the skip due to excessive oil on the ropes which was causing the skip to slip back down the shaft.

There was 39 ton drawn on the Monday, nothing on Tuesday and nothing on Wednesday. The checkweighman went down the pit. The new weigh machine which is down the pit weighs two mine cars at a time. Average weight of coal in cars 3 tons (app). Weight of mining car without coal one ton ten cwt one quarter. After the Theresa site skips had been inspected by J.Daves and N. Young it was passed safe for man riding. This to be operated while H.S. side is being changed from steam to electric'.

The change-over was not without casualties. The introduction of powerloading faces under ground reduced the number of men required to work at the coal face. At first the miners' lodge was given a figure of 190 to be made redundant but after negotiations some men were found jobs on the new washer at bank, and in the event only 64 men lost their jobs.

The toll of accidents however continued as the lodge diary again informs us:

'On Monday morning April 25 1960 Geo. Armstrong and his marrow Ralph Grieves, both bargain men, were working at a bordroom in the 4th East District of the Low Main Seam.

They had just rid out some stone and were preparing to end a strap to secure the working place when a fall of stone occurred.

It dislodged the prop and strap already set

Dawdon colliery 1974

and it pinned R.Grieves by the head and shoulders to the floor. With assistance he was freed within seconds but when brought to the surface he was found to be dead.

Ralph was a single person who resided with his older brother Joe.

Coroners verdict (Accidental Death)'.

It was not just Dawdon's physical profile that changed in the 1960s. The composition of its workforce was also changing. As the decade progressed more and more collieries were closed in the west and central areas of the Durham coalfield and Dawdon became one of the principal receiving collieries for the men displaced from these pits. Many of the newcomers had worked all their lives in the narrow seams of the west and found the high seams difficult to get used to. It was not an uncommon sight to see these men filling coal on their knees on a six-feet-high coal face.

The introduction of power-loading faces and then in 1966 the national power-loading agreement finally brought to an end piece work and therefore pay that was negotiated at pit level. Dawdon had now to fall in line with the rest of the county and receive the standard rate of pay.

By 1969 miners' pay was clearly falling behind the rates that were being paid in other industries, particularly the wages paid to men working at bank. In 1969 an unofficial strike started in the Doncaster area over this very issue, and Dawdon colliery was one of the three mines in the Durham area that responded to this call and took part in the action.

Again in 1971 dissatisfaction with the general level of payments resulted in strike action in Yorkshire, and Dawdon, ever true to its militant tradition, joined them. These strikes were the unofficial precursor to the 1972 and 74 official strikes, which went some way to restoring miners' position in the earnings league.

In 1974 Dawdon was preparing to strike out to a new area of coal which had been discovered six kilometres out under the North Sea. It was to be a joint project with Vane Tempest colliery which lay a mile and a half to the north of Dawdon colliery on the other side of the Seaham fault. Each colliery was to drive a main roadway six miles out under the sea. Once into the coal these roadways would be joined to form the main infrastructure of the new district.

A new German tunnelling machine called The Mole was brought to Dawdon colliery to drive the main drift. This formidable machine filled the whole roadway with rotating cutting heads that eroded the stone as it advanced. Unfortunately problems were encountered from the outset, due in part to the Mole's sheer weight and in part to the weak floor of the drivage. However these problems paled into insignificance as the project developed when in 1975 it was discovered that the coal seam was taking the drivages dangerously close to the sea bed. No one had suspected the existence of an antipode, a dome shaped fault which threw the seams upward.

Although a plan to circumnavigate the domes was considered, the NCB decided that it would be too costly and that the coal could be in the future exploited by Easington colliery, which had been sunk six miles to the south of Dawdon. This was for the long-term future of Dawdon a devastating blow. Suddenly Dawdon colliery was no longer immortal, and the realisation began to grow that this coal machine had a finite future. Landward expansion was blocked by the workings of other collieries, Vane Tempest to the north and Easington to the south. Seaham was working to the west as was Murton. In seam C Murton was

C 12 face installation, Dawdon colliery, July 1990.
Left to right : John W. Reeve; chock fitter, Tommy Wilson; Powerloader ,Brian Little; chock fitter, Keith Alan;Powerloader.
Photo: John W. Reeve.

Dawdon miners marching back to work after 1984/85 strike

within 600yds of Dawdon's shafts. Even so it was still thought that abundant reserves were available to be exploited between the domes and the land in the G, E and C seams.

The miners' union at Dawdon, while disturbed by this change in fortunes, was still confident that the reserves were adequate if properly managed to satisfy production for many decades. By 1984 and the start of the year-long strike against pit closures, Dawdon miners in common with those of the other large coastal collieries saw their participation in the struggle more from the point of view of assisting other collieries than that of securing a future for their own colliery. Dawdon

miners after a moment's hesitation came crashing down on the side of the strike with all its tradition of solidarity and militancy.

The women, organised in the Save Easington Area Mines (SEAM) campaign, provided a kitchen in the Welfare Hall serving the families with hot meals throughout the year.

There were also casualties, and five Dawdon men were sentenced to two years in prison.

Two Dawdon men were to have a significant influence on the transformation of the Area leadership of the NUM from 'moderate. to 'left'. Billy Etherington, the Dawdon Mechanics delegate, was elected to the position of Area

Photo: Keith Pattison

Dawdon lodge banner at Durham Big Meeting 1985

Secretary of the Durham Colliery Mechanics Association just prior to the 1984 strike, and David Guy, the treasurer of the miners' lodge, was elected President of the Durham Area in 1986.

It was not long after the return to work in 1985 that Dawdon began to experience problems. Confined to a relatively small area and working three different levels created the inevitable difficulties of working under seams from which the coal had been extracted. In November 1986 the E90s area suffered an inrush of water that eventually settled at a rate of inflow of 450 galls/minute. To cope with this water the range in the shaft had to be upgraded to 1200 galls/min.

When the water was analysed to trace its origins it was calculated that 75 per cent was from the Permian strata. This effectively ended any hope of E90s development as management judged that the mine would not be able to handle another inrush of these proportions.

In an effort to discover if it was possible to develop faces to the south of the E90 area an exploratory drift was driven upwards from 18 South roadway in a north-easterly direction. In 150yds the roadway passed through many faults and encountered water from the Seaham Fault.

In view of all these problems it was concluded in December 1988 that there were no workable reserves in the E90s area.

In the same year in the G seam the unions were faced with the classic mining "catch 22" situation where jobs are counterpoised to safety.

The proposed G80 and G81 development lay beneath a massive pond of water in the E80 area just 35ft above. Management calculated that this pond probably contained 11 million gallons of water, and drove a series of bore holes at different angles up to drain the water. In total 15 million gallons of water were drained from the area before the holes were sealed. It was then calculated by management that the pond had returned to its original level.

After the Lofthouse disaster, in which 30 men were drowned in an inrush of water, more strict legislation was passed by Parliament to require a manager to satisfy himself that no inrush of water will occur. The manager decided in the interests of safety that one million tons of reserves should be abandoned. While this was a severe blow to the job prospects of their members the union could only agree that safety was the more important.

This incident transformed Dawdon colliery to a one-seam colliery with all its workable reserves in the C seam.

In February 1989 British Coal announced its intention to work the 3.8 million tons of coal in seam C at the rate of 4,000 saleable tons per day, employing 1,000 men, projecting a four-year life for the colliery. In the event, the thinning of the seams reduced this prediction by 18 months and the colliery was closed in July 1991.

Easington colliery 1915

EASINGTON COLLIERY

On a November day in 1899, Miss Barwick of Thimberly Hall cut the first sod of the North pit at Easington colliery. The expansion of the Durham coalfield was now in its final phase.

It was planned that the colliery was to have two shafts, a North downcast shaft and a South upcast shaft.

A French sinking company was engaged to freeze the water and sand below the limestone. The company's technique, however, proved inadequate to the task, and the coal company was forced to dispense with their services and engage

a Belgium firm who recommenced the sinking of the South shaft.

In 1904 the water again broke into the shaft. At first it was thought that the inrush could be contained, and two of the three men working in the shaft were dispatched to bank to get a pump. The third man, a Mr. R Atkinson of Kelloe, stayed at the bottom of the shaft in order to guide the kibble on its return. Suddenly the inrush turned into an inundation and Atkinson was drowned and his body lost. This halted the sinking of the shaft and the Belgians, having fared no better than the

French, were dismissed. The Easington Coal Company was by now bankrupt and it was not until 1907 that the company was effectively taken over by the Weardale Steel, Coal and Coke Company, although the old company was to retain its name. Now German engineers were engaged to resume the sinking using a more advanced method of freezing. As they began the excavation of the South shaft they found the body of Atkinson frozen in a block of ice. Three years after he was drowned his body was removed and taken to Kelloe for burial.

To ease the pressure of the sand feeder on the sinking a third shaft, the West pit, was sunk 450ft to the sand bed and a dump drift was driven from the shaft at 200ft to the beach where the water was discharged into the sea.

On September 17 1909 the North shaft at last bottomed out at a depth of 1,585ft at the Hutton seam, with a finished diameter of 20ft, a considerable size for its time.

Up to this point in time the village of Easington colliery did not exist. The rudimentary dwellings of the sinkers perched on that windswept spot above the North Sea were all that existed of a settlement. Now that coal had been reached the pit rows were constructed with a sense of urgency.

On February 21 1910 the pit buzzer was sounded for the first time as the South shaft was bottomed out 200ft below the Hutton seam with a

Easinton sinking during freezing process 1902

finished diameter of 20ft. The first districts were quickly won by July, and by September the first coals were brought to bank via the North pit. It was to be a year later that the South pit was fully fitted out for coal work.

As the company built its village hugging the extremities of the pit yard the houses filled with miners' families who came from all over Durham and the surrounding counties. Many came from Ireland and Wales.

In July 1912, the community was beginning to look like a real village. In the same month the Railway Station opened for passengers, a Working Men's club admitted its first members and the miners Hall was opened, as was the Empire cinema. Before the year was out the Black Diamond Hotel was added to the list of watering holes to tempt the miners of the new colliery.

The close proximity of the houses to the pit was not unusual in a colliery village, however in 1913 it was demonstrated how potentially dangerous this particular feature of the miners' life could be.

It was the time of year when the cage rope in the South pit had to be changed. It was the practice when changing a rope to rest the one cage on girders placed across the shaft at an inset while the other cage was at rest at the bottom of the shaft. On this occasion the rope was uncoupled from the lower cage and the winder was used to raise the other cage while the girder was removed. The assumption had been made that the winder could

Sinkers at Easington colliery 1900

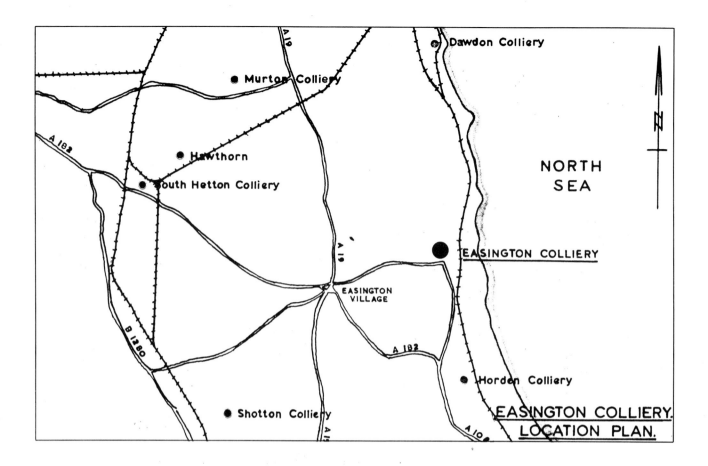

NORTH
SEA

EASINGTON COLLIERY.
LOCATION PLAN.

hold the upper cage without the counterbalance of the lower cage.

The assumption proved erroneous and the upper cage plummeted down the shaft, dragging the rope with it. In the opposite side of the shaft the other end of the rope, now freed from the lower cage, came hurtling up the shaft with a fearsome acceleration and on reaching the pulley wheels was travelling with such speed and momentum that the rope wrapped round the girders of the headgear. The girders were torn from their housings and propelled high over the pit yard like a missile from some huge medieval siege machine. One girder crashed through the roof of a house in First Street East, smashing through the ceiling of the bedroom and into the bed, while the second crashed through the wall into the front room of the same house. The bed was shared by two brothers who worked alternate shifts, giving it a three-to-one chance of being occupied at the time of the accident. Fortunately for Joe and Ben Egglestone, neither was in bed at the time; the former was down the pit while the latter had decided to visit relatives.

As the scale of the mines working's increased the

output of the colliery steadily rose, reaching a peak of 1,053,453 tons per annum in 1929. By this time there were 1,400 hewers and putters working in-bye extracting the coal, mainly by hand. But this was the year of the Wall Street crash and the beginning of the depression that was to make its mark in Easington when in 1933 families were leaving the village in search of work. The closure of the Main Coal seam had caused wide-scale redundancies.

In 1931 an aerial flight was constructed to tip the colliery waste on to the beach, a practice that was to prove controversial to the day the colliery closed.

The 30s was a decade of depression and hardship throughout Durham, but in Easington there was a little comfort when in 1934 a new miners' hall was opened to replace the original which had been destroyed by fire in 1929. In 1935 the Main Coal was re-entered and in 1937 the first pit baths were opened.

The end of the decade brought new dangers with the start of the Second World War. Perched on the cliff top the colliery was an easy target for German bombers and in 1940 the pit sidings were bombed, killing eight men.

One year later in 1941 the cage rope in the North pit cage snapped and the cage plunged to the bottom of the shaft. The unthinkable had happened but mercifully no one was in the cage at the time.

Easington colliery 1920, with West pit in foreground

By 1944, after four years of arduous production under the discipline of the Emergency Powers Act (EPA) the strain between men and managers was beginning to tell. In January of that year the miners of Easington colliery risked being jailed under the EPA, which made striking illegal, when they struck work for a week in a wages dispute, and in March 450 putters operated a go slow.

Better times were not far away and on January 1st 1947 Easington miner's celebrated the best new year's day of their lives, the beginning of the era of nationalisation.

At this time the colliery was employing mining methods that two decades before were regarded as advanced, but were now inadequate for the high-production, long-life colliery that was planned by the new administration. The old system of 10cwt tubs and hand-filling faces was to be replaced by fully mechanised faces and a coal transport system utilising conveyer belts and 2.8 ton mine cars. The shaft cages were to be changed in order that both shafts could raise these new mine cars .

The preliminary work on this change-over had just begun when at shortly before five a.m. on June 29 1951, just as the night shift men were being relieved by the first shift, an explosion ripped through the Five Quarter Duck Bill district of Easington colliery with devastating consequences.

Goerge Ottowell, was 27 and a permanent member of the Crook Rescue Brigade. He had been raised from his bed at the brigade headquarters at five and by six am had travelled 20 miles and was passing through the large crowd assembled at the gates of the pit. He was to recall that moment 42 years later:

> ' I can see their faces as if it was today. They were looking up at us hoping we could do something. I remember thinking to myself, I'm in a better position than those poor people, at least I can do something, they can only stand there and wait.'

The rescue brigades in Northumberland and Durham were organised around three permanent centres. In Durham the Houghton-le-Spring Brigade covered the miners on the East coast while the Crook Rescue Brigade covered the pits to the West. In Northumberland a brigade stationed at Benwell Towers in Newcastle covered the South of that county while the Ashington-based brigade covered the north.

If disaster struck in the Houghton Brigade's area then they were immediately mobilised and the next district, Crook, was put on alert as the second call brigade; Benwell would be the third call and Ashington the fourth. In addition to the full-time brigades each pit had its own team of part-time brigades men, known as the Fire and Rescue Teams. These men were volunteers and received six training sessions a year to keep them conversant with the arduous task of travelling and working while wearing the cumbersome breathing apparatus.

In 1951 the breathing apparatus available to the brigades was primitive compared to that which is available today. It consisted of a heavy harness supporting a back pack containing liquid oxygen. The apparatus was known officially as the 'Brown Hills Self Contained Breathing Apparatus' and weighed 39lbs. As the liquid evaporated it was controlled by a valve and a breathing bag that inflated as the operator breathed in through a mouthpiece. A non-return valve ensured that the operator could breathe out without the spent oxygen coming into contact with the oxygen in the breathing bag.

Once in a district laden with poisonous gases the rescuer had a maximum of two hours to work before all the liquid oxygen was spent. It was vital that the nose clip and mouth piece were firmly in place all the time as just one breath of the lethal gas could overpower the rescuer.

The two main gasses generated in an explosion are carbon monoxide (after damp) and carbon

From left to right: G. Vayro, D. Edwards, G. Ottowell and R. Dent of the Crook Permanent Rescue Brigade, Fire officer of Dean and Chapter colliery and three members of the colliery volunteer brigade. Photographed before training exercise at Dean and Chapter colliery 1951. Photo: G. Ottowell.

dioxide (black damp). The former is highly toxic and combines with the blood, killing in a few seconds. Only one per cent of the air in a district has to be contaminated to prove fatal. The latter is not poisonous and is present in fresh air. However if an explosion uses up all the oxygen in the atmosphere and only carbon dioxide remains then life cannot be supported and any unfortunate miner left there would be suffocated.

One of the most efficient tests for these gases was a canary in a cage. These small birds react seven times more quickly than human beings to the existence of lethal gases, wobbling or falling off their perches.

The brigaders' liquid oxygen was produced by a liquefaction plant at the rescue station and stored in large vacuum flasks. These flasks were extremely heavy and had usually to be carried by hand. To fill the breathing apparatus a tripod would be erected on which the apparatus was weighed. The exact amount of the liquid was then poured into the oxygen compartment, carefully preventing any spilling and contact with the skin of the operator.

In order to communicate when wearing the breathing apparatus the brigaders used hooters. Two members of the six man teams had a hooter operated with one hand. It was tied by a lariat round the neck. One blast on the hooter was a distress call, two blasts to halt, three to retire, four to advance and five to call attention.

Once at the scene of a disaster the first call team would descend the mine and establish a fresh air base as close to the seat of the explosion as possible. This would be an area where the ventilation of the pit was unaffected or where it could be easily restored by erecting temporary brattice partitions. The fresh air base would become the control centre for the rescue. Here the liquid oxygen would be stored, tea and food would be available and a doctor would be in attendance. Towards the accident an advanced base was established from which the rescuers entered the operation area. By the time the first team was into the operation area the second call team would be waiting at the advance base, the third would be at the fresh air base and the fourth would be waiting at bank.

After two hours of arduous labour in the operation area the first team's oxygen would be exhausted and they would retire to the advance base where they would brief the incoming team. At the fresh air base a longer consultation would take place before they returned to bank and back to the rescue station. They would then relieve the stand-by team that had remained at the rescue station in the event of there being a emergency at a second pit.

As George Ottowell was preparing to go underground at Easington colliery, Steve Cummings, a colliery fore-overman and captain of the Murton Colliery Fire and Rescue Team, was 1,100ft underground in the Third East District of the Five Quarter seam at Murton colliery when he was informed by the colliery surveyor of the Easington explosion.

He was told to report to the colliery manager who relieved him of all his duties and placed him on stand-by to go to Easington when called.

At Easington it was quickly established that 81 men were unaccounted for and that the ventilation in the district had completely broken down.

At seven-thirty a.m. George Ottowell had reached the fresh air station, charged his breathing apparatus and advanced into the operation zone with four other members of the Crook rescue brigade. He recalls:

Your first duty is to look for any signs of life; the thought that someone may be alive is what drives you on. We were not long in the district when we heard heavy breathing and discovered a young miner. Despite the weight of the apparatus we were carrying we were running to get him out to the doctor at the fresh air base. You see it's the thought that you can save a life that pumps the adrenaline into your body.'

Matt Williams, the 18-year-old loader lad, left the pit alive but sadly did not survive the journey to hospital.

By the afternoon of June 29 Steve Cummings had been instructed to report to Easington colliery at five am on Wednesday. He had been told that the Easington rescuer, Jack Wallace, with whom he had been training two weeks previously, had collapsed and died 100 yds into the disaster area. Jack was just 26 years old.

As Steve climbed on to the tarpaulin-covered lorry that was to take him to Easington he had plenty of time to reflect on what might have happened to his friend. Perhaps, he considered, his mouthpiece had been dislodged from his mouth. Once through the sombre crowd at the pit

gates Steve could see the huge pit yard thronging with activity. The central workshop had been made the cover base for the rescue teams. Here was the control room for the organisation of the underground recovery operations. In one room a doctor was examining every member of the rescue teams before they prepared to go underground, and in the yard were several mobile laboratories where samples of the air taken from the stricken district and from the mines return airways were being analysed. All kinds of rescue equipment was stacked in every available space.

The pace at which the rescue teams were being dispatched underground had been increased to one every half hour. Now, after the loss of a brigadesman, every team on the move in the operation zone had to be covered by a second team. At the time Steve had reached the mine there were three teams waiting to go underground.

On a normal day, waiting to go underground is a light-hearted time, a time to recount the previous day's gossip and share a joke. But now the atmosphere was tense, the mood sombre, conversation confined to the job in hand. The Great Northern coalfield was doing what it had done on so many occasions. No appeals for volunteers had to be made, the men to do the job were at hand, their whole life in a mining community a preparation for task they were now performing.

Steve's team consisted of G. R. Davidson, C. Prescod. J. Brown, G. Monarch and his vice-captain A. Graham.

After carefully checking their breathing apparatus they descended the downcast shaft to a depth of 1,000ft to the Main Coal level, from which they travelled 400yds north to the junction of the road into the Five-Quarter District (West). This road was blocked by a 200yd fall of stone caused by the explosion, and the team had to continue north for a further 600 yds along a drift into the Seven Quarter District.

On entering the Seven Quarter return airway they travelled 600yds west and then still in the return they travelled 300yds south to where a fresh air base had been established on the edge of the disaster area. It was here that Steve Cummings was re-acquainted with the Superintendent of the Crook Rescue Brigade, Jim Richardson. Jim had trained Steve 12 years previously and they had both been on duty at the Murton explosion in 1942 when 13 men lost their lives.

By now, all knew that there was little chance of finding any one alive unless by a freak of nature a pocket of fresh air, large enough to support life, had been isolated from the main body of stagnant lethal gas. The main task of the teams was to restore the ventilation so that the sad task of recovering the bodies could be completed.

The team was given the task of advancing into the district to the No. 7 heading, where they were to replace a brick stopping, which had been blown away in the blast, with a temporary stopping made of brattice cloth.

On their way along what had been the main airway of the Five-Quarter district they passed a victim slumped over the belt, his back pierced by a flying object. They continued on and after negotiating two fairly minor roof-falls found themselves at the entrance to the 125hp main-and-tail hauler engine house. Here were a further three victims sitting together and looking quite normal apart from each having a rosy complexion, the definite sign of carbon monoxide poisoning. It was clear that death had come to these men so swiftly that they had little knowledge of what was happening.

As Steve's team continued in-bye they encountered two more victims under a roof-fall. This part of the roadway was supported by wooden props, with straight girders against the roof, many of which had been dislodged by the blast. The belt structure was twisted across the roadway and tubs had been derailed and overturned.

By now the 44lbs of safety harness and oxygen were weighing heavily on the shoulders of the team members. Each was sweating profusely, to such an extent that the map in Steve Cummings' pocket was soaked and the marks on it were becoming illegible. Now they were in the greatest danger negotiating a path over the belt structure and fallen girders. As their strength waned any careless movement or a fall of stone from the unsupported parts of the roadway could easily cause their nose clips or mouthpieces to become dislodged, with disastrous consequences.

Having got through the worst of the fall they were alerted by distress signals in advance of them. Hurrying forward they came across a rescuer in a severely agitated state. They communicated by chalking on the side of a tub and were able to discover that this was a member of a team of five that had split up into a party of two and three so that they might complete their task more easily. When one of the two parties failed to meet at the arranged time panic set in and this man had been sent out to get assistance. Steve and his team set off in search of the missing men. They had not proceeded far when they were relieved to see lights coming towards them out of the darkness. They

Easington people with Lord Hyndley, chairman of NCB 1951

were united with the missing team just at the spot where Jack Wallace had collapsed and died the previous evening.

After satisfying themselves that the men of the advance team were composed enough to travel out-bye without assistance Steve and the Murton team turned to completing their assignment.

Turning west they penetrated further into the disaster zone until they came upon No. 10 heading, where they erected a canvas stopping, leaving a gap of three feet as they had been instructed. Now they returned to No. 9 stopping where they completed a partly built stopping. This allowed a current of air to penetrate further into the district flowing into the returns via No. 10 heading. Their task completed the party returned to the fresh air base where they gave their report.

This was typical of the dangerous and painstaking work of the brigades men. By the time they got back to bank they had spent eight hours at the mine. It was now only a day and a half after the fatal blast. 16 of the 81 missing men had been located and one rescuer had been added to the death list.

As the rescue brigade advanced the ventilation an army of miners came in their wake, repairing the damaged roadways and constructing more permanent stoppings.

Steve and his team returned to the mine at 3.00 a.m. on June 31st and were subject to a rigorous medical before being allowed underground. The strain was beginning to tell on many of the rescuers and 20 had failed the medical that day. In the event all of Steve's team were passed as fit.

The fresh air base had now been advanced further in-bye to No. 16 heading and a cover base had been established at No. 7. Steve was astounded by the amount of repair work that had been achieved. The whole 200 yds of the fall on the road from the Seven Quarter had been timbered above the fall.

They reached the cover base at 8.00 a.m. where they found three rescue teams wrapped in blankets as protection against the cold and damp. Their mission on this occasion was to cover a team of technicians who were taking samples of air further in-bye, making sure that they got out safely. This was to be the easiest operation they were called upon to perform. The next was to prove far more arduous.

It was 10 a.m. on June 1 when the Murton team were next on duty. As they turned into the street alongside the colliery they were halted by a great crowd of people. For 80yds their vehicle slowly edged its way through the throng and into the pit gates. A second rescue worker had been killed and rumours of a second explosion had quickly spread through the village, emptying the houses of the grieving community.

The team were quickly examined and passed fit for duty. They sat down with three or four other teams to assess the mornings event's. Steve Cummings later wrote:

'Worry and panic could be felt all around, only sitting around the stove with my fellow Colliery Rescue Workers did I feel proud to be a member of such a body of men, calm and cool, just waiting to be called for duty, knowing that our only job was recovery of the victims for a decent burial.'

On arrival at the fresh air base at No. 19 stenton Steve and his team learned that the exploration of the district had been suspended.

Up to this time the priority had been the restoration of the ventilation, allowing the teams to penetrate deeper into the disaster zone and identify where all the victims were. Now it was apparent that having to pass the bodies of the victims, already dead for three days, was having a debilitating effect on the members of the brigades. It was therefore agreed that each team would recover a body.

As Steve and his team entered the zone their attention was caught by the frantic distress calls on the hooters of the advance team. With the tragic events of that morning fresh in mind, their pace quickened. Thirty yards on they came upon the advance team. One member was lying face down on the floor. Two were sitting on the belt with what looked like a grinning expression on their faces. Two others were standing where a body had been tipped off a stretcher, appealing for help.

Shaking the men on the belt into sensibility, they motioned to them to get on their feet and get out of the district. Four of the Murton team each grabbed a limb of the collapsed man, placed him on the stretcher and carried him out-bye. Where the roof was less than five feet high they were reduced to dragging the stretcher while crawling on their knees.

Once at the fresh air base the collapsed man and the rest of the team were treated with a Novita recovery apparatus. The stricken brigades man was handed to the carrying team who rushed him to bank. He was taken to Ryhope hospital and given a blood transfusion and later removed to Newcastle, where a second blood transfusion was administered. There is no doubt that the remarkable speed of this recovery saved the life of this brave man.

Steve and his team were to re-enter the disaster zone on two more occasions that day to help in the removal of the bodies.

In all between May 29 and June 7 when the ventilation was finally restored to the whole district Steve Cummings and his team were on duty on eight occasions. Although the whole team at times suffered side affects of their arduous task they kept their own council and presented themselves for their medical each time they were called.

There were six men and their story could be repeated a hundred times over by the miners who without consideration for their own lives answered the call when this terrible disaster occurred at Easington colliery.

The years that have passed have not diminished the grief felt for the victims or the admiration we have for the brave men of the rescue brigades.

It was not until a year later that work on the reorganisation of the colliery was recommended. By 1958 the colliery was virtually unrecognisable. The entire surface plant had been electrified, eliminating 19 Lancaster boilers and all the steam-driven compressors. Now each shaft was served by a 2,500 hp Met. Vick/ Markham winder on the Ward-Leonard system.

Underground trunk belts were installed to take the coal from in-bye to loading points where it was filled into 2.8 ton mine cars. These mine cars were raised through the shaft in double-decked cages each carrying two cars. Both North and South shafts were used for the riding of men, coal, and supplies.

IN MEMORIAM

JOHN ANSON	THOMAS EDWARD JONES
WILLIAM ARMSTRONG	JOHN KELLY
MARK SMART BEDDING	WILLIAM KELLY
MATTHEW BLEVINS	JOHN EDWARD ARMSTRONG LAMB
GEORGE BRENKLEY	JESSE STEPHENSON LINK
THOMAS BRENKLEY	JOSEPH FAIRLESS LIPPEATT
LOUIS BRENNAN	PETER LYNCH
GEORGE MILLER BROWN	DENIS McROY
HENRY BURDESS	WILLIAM JAMES McROY
BERTRAM BURN	ROBERT WILLIAM MILBURN
EMMERSON CAIN	HAROLD NELSON
FREDERICK CAIRNS	ALBERT NEWCOMBE
GEORGE CALVERT	NORMAN NICHOLSON
JAMES CALVIN	ROBERT NOBLE
FREDERICK CARR	WILLIAM EDWARD FORBES PARKS
GEORGE WILLIAM CARR	WILLIAM PARKIN
JAMES CARR	ROBERT PASE
JOHN EDWIN CHALLONER	STANLEY PEACEFUL
RICHARD CHAMPLEY	ALEXANDER PENMAN
JOSEPH CHARLTON	JAMES PORTER
ALBERT KERR CHAPMAN	JOHN THOMAS PORTER
JOHN CLOUGH	THOMAS VALENTINE RICE
WILLIAM ARTHUR DRYDEN	JOHN ROBINSON
JOHN ELLISON	JOHN GEORGE ROBSON
CHARLES FISHBURN	GEORGE SCOTT
HENRY FISHBURN	ALBERT SEYMOUR
THOMAS GARSIDE	FREDERICK SILLITO
JOSEPH GODSMAN	GEORGE HENRY STUBBS
ALBERT GOWLAND	MATTHEW WHITE SURTEES
GEORGE GOULBURN	HUGH BELL SURTEES
ERNEST GOYNS	LAURENCE THOMPSON
HERBERT GOYNS	THOMAS THOMPSON
JOHN HARKER	THOMAS TRISNAN
JOHN WILLIAM HENDERSON	ROBERT TURNBULL
THOMAS HEPPLE	JACK YOUNG WALLACE
DANIEL HUNT	GEORGE WILKIE
STEPHEN HUNT	REGINALD WILKINSON
WILLIAM HUNT	MATTHEW WILLIAMS
ARTHUR CHAMBERS HUTTON	ROBERT WILLINS
FREDERICK ERNEST JEPSON	JOHN WILSON
HERBERT JEFFREY JOBLING	STEPHEN WILSON
LAWRENCE JONES	

' Let light perpetual shine upon them '

Victims of the disaster, from memorial service hymn sheet

The West pit heapstead was dismantled and the shaft capped.

The new coal preparation plant could handle 500 tons of coal per hour and graded coal in six different sizes up to six inches.

Pneumatic power was delivered underground from a power house where directly coupled electrical motors drove the compressors.

The colliery was now organised underground from two horizons, the upper at 900ft and the lower at 1300ft. From the loading points in each horizon the mine cars were hauled to the shaft in 40 car sets by battery and diesel driven locomotives. At the shaft area the mine cars were transferred to a pneumatically powered clearance system, which loaded the cars into the cage using rams.

In the course of the reorganisation no fewer than 15 miles of return airways had been enlarged and lined to improve the ventilation system in-bye.

Of Easington's five principal seams which extended out under the sea the furthest workings were now four miles out.

In 1958 the colliery was producing 872,000 tons of coal per year, an output per man-shift (OMS) of 24.6cwt; just under 3,300 tons per day; an overall OMS of one ton.

In 1956 a Huwood slice loader was introduced into the Low Main seam (J). This unusual coal getting machine had been developed at Washington F colliery. The slice loader was a development of the coal plough modified especially for faces where the coal was considered too hard for a conventional plough. Two oscillating blades at either end of the machine are fitted with picks which shear the coal from the face in an oscillating movement as the machine is hauled up the face. This innovation however does not appear to have proved successful enough to

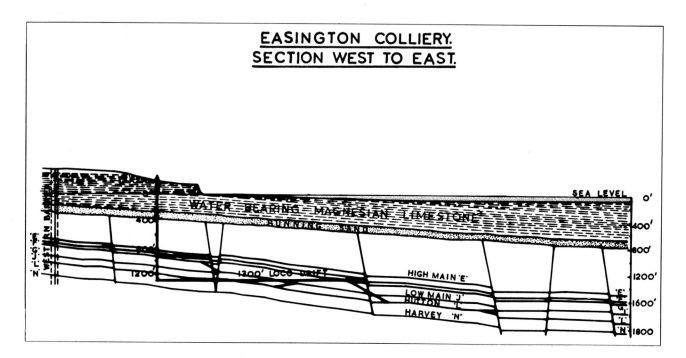

74

Typical return airway before enlargement

Typical return airway after enlargement

be adopted as an alternative to shearing.

By 1966 Easington was a principal coal producer in the county, producing in excess of 5,000 tons of coal per day, the product of six longwall shearer faces and six continuous miners. In the High Main seam, which was six foot thick, two longwall advancing faces were producing 3,400 tons per day. The balance was produced in the Main seam (F) and the Low Main (J) seams. In this year the colliery produced 1,191,907 tons of coal, an output per man-shift of 44.9 cwts.

In 1978 the last major development of the pit was effected when the North pit was converted to skip winding. The new headgears required for skip winding changed the profile of the colliery for the last time. The air flow was reversed and the North pit, formerly the downcast shaft became the upcast shaft and was fitted with two 1,800 KW Keith Blackman Radial Flow fans. While one fan was in operation the other was standing by. Coal was

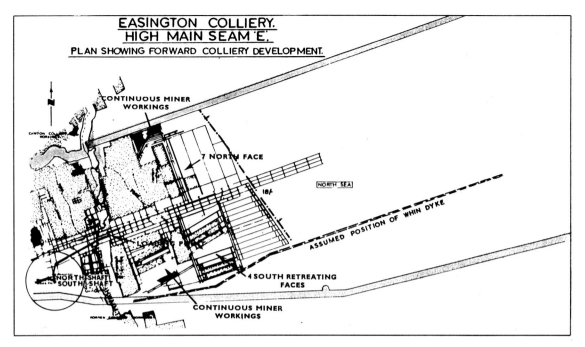

EASINGTON COLLIERY.
HIGH MAIN SEAM 'E.'
PLAN SHOWING FORWARD COLLIERY DEVELOPMENT.

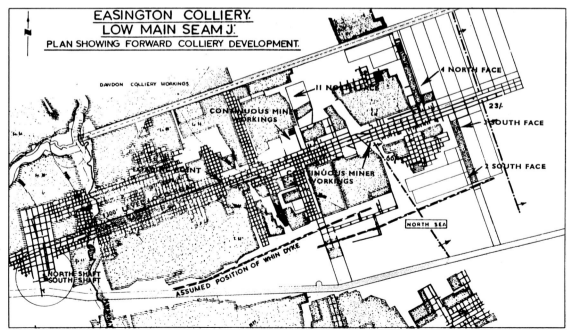

EASINGTON COLLIERY.
LOW MAIN SEAM 'J.'
PLAN SHOWING FORWARD COLLIERY DEVELOPMENT.

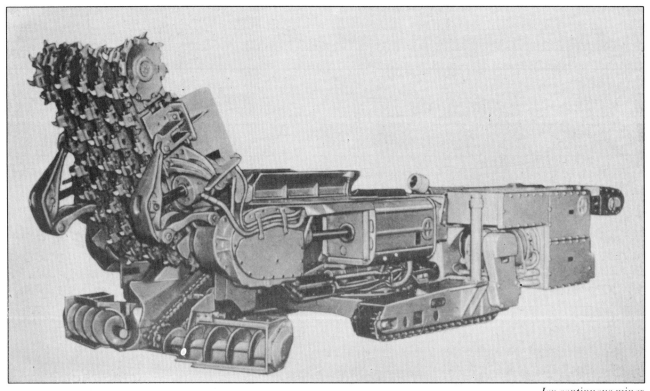

Joy continuous miner

now being extracted from the High Main (E), Main Coal (F2), Yard (G) and the Low Main (J).

For many years Easington colliery was regarded as a militant pit. It had joined with Dawdon colliery in the unofficial wages strikes in 1969 and 1971. In 1972 and 1974 the union lodge under the leadership of Redvers Garside had taken a leading role in the organisation of the picketing of the Teeside fuel depots.

In 1983 the chairman of the lodge Billy Stobbs was the first rank-and-file-miner in the

Huwood slicer loader in operation

area to be elected to the National Executive of the NUM.

In 1984 Easington was one of the first collieries to respond to the call for a national strike against pit closures, although few doubted that Easington colliery itself was quite safe from closure. Although there were many men who travelled to the pit from the surrounding villages, Easington was still very much a village pit and retained all the traditions of loyalty to the union and aversion to any individual who dared go to work when the men were on strike.

The strike was by no means solely the preserve of the men of the village. For months before, the women of the village had taken part in the Save Easington Area Mines (SEAM) campaign, and within weeks of the strike starting had organised a feeding centre, in the Colliery club, the first to

Easington colliery management and trade union representatives, October 1958.
Back row: W. Thrower, Manager, G. Dunn Chair. DEA, A. Wilson Sec. DEA, T. Blackburn Chair NACODs,
R. Hunter Chair COSA, J. Reynolds sec NUM.
Front row: J.G. Tebbs Group Manager, T. Nicholson Sec DCMA, J. Williams Sec COSA, J. Pearson chair DCMA,
R. Merrington Sec. NACODs, C. Quinn Chair NUM.

Looking from loco sheds before modernisation, 1974

Photo: C. Stout

Installing north headgear 1976

Photo: C. Stout

North headgear completed 1977

be established in the county. This was no soup kitchen. As Heather Wood, one of the leaders of the movement always insisted, it was 'a free cafe for miners and their families'. Each shop in the village donated something towards the effort and soon the cafe was sustaining 500 hot meals per day and many food parcels for the single men.

In August of that year the Coal Board made its second attempt to persuade men to return to work. Their first attempt on July 9th had been a total failure. At Easington the colliery manager Peter Farrage assured the union that at his colliery any man who returned to work would have to walk through the main gate of the colliery yard under his own steam. The local lodges of the union took the manager at his word and on the Sunday night of August 19 resorted to the simple solution of barricading the main gate to the colliery with a collection of armoured face conveyers and oil drums. They were quite confident no one was going to try to return but it was just as well to be sure. This was the start of what was to prove the

Photo: Keith Pattison   *Miners and their families in free cafe at Colliery Club 1984*

most violent week in the history of Easington colliery. The following is a personal sketch of the events of that week:

Monday August 20 was the day the Coal Board arranged for the pit buses to bring any would-be blackleg to the pit. If they worked for a week they would receive their holiday pay, several hundred pounds, after six months without wages a veritable fortune.

That Monday morning Office Street is packed with pickets waiting for the back-shift bus. There had been rumours that a traveller from Durham was going to attempt to get in.

When the bus finally arrives, it is confirmed; a miner is on the bus. He is carefully shepherded off by the police who form a wedge shape around him. Union officials approach to reason with him but their advances are rebuffed by the police.

In an attempt to clear a path to the main gate the police advance the wedge and push into the body of pickets defending the gate. A sudden flurry of activity erupts, helmets fly into the air, as men arriving from Hordon and Murton swell the ranks of the pickets.

On this occasion the police, heavily

Poto: W. Stobbs

Office Street

Poto: W. Stobbs

A sudden flurry of activity

outnumbered are forced to retreat. The blackleg is bundled into a police van and removed from the village.

The next day, the blackleg returns but is met at Easington village by men who, like him, had been recently transferred from the closed Kelloe pit. They try to reason with him. This time he hasn't got his bait bag with him and he returns home to his village.

Wednesday and Thursday pass without incident. Piers Merchant, the Tory MP from Newcastle, has complained that the police are

not making the same effort to bring the blackleg in at Easington as they are at Wearmouth.

Friday morning: there are many more police at the colliery, police from Gwent in Wales and Northampton. Office Street is again tightly packed with pickets; men have come from Murton, Dawdon and Hordon to ensure that the line is not breached at Easington. The atmosphere is tense.

On the steps of the colliery office the local MP Jack Dorman can be seen with Billy

Stobbs, the lodge chairman, and Alan Cummings, the lodge secretary. Out of sight, behind the huge baths complex the car park is filling with police in riot gear. Suddenly the throng of pickets is alive with rumours, some one says 'he's in; they've taken him in through the baths'. They surge forward to where Billy Stobbs has climbed the steps to the colliery office. There he turns to face the strained faces of the miners.

'Its true he's in, but me and Jack Dormond are going in to see the manager and to get him to stick to his word about the main gate.' Tension mounts as they wait. The only sound is a low murmur of discontent. The disturbed faces of the young men show it all. A group of them stand by the railings in front of the huts on the east side of the colliery offices. The railings bar their way into the pit yard. They are grasping the six foot high railings in their clenched fists drawing them towards them testing their strength.

Billy Stobbs appears again on the top of the office steps. The murmur of the waiting pickets rises in pitch, now resembling the buzz of a angry hive of bees. Billy holds up his arm as he begins to tell them that the manager has been overruled from Area. Area says the

Poto: W. Stobbs

Police in riot gear file into pit yard

blackleg has to stay at the pit at all costs. Billy's hand remains aloft, the palm towards the crowd as if to restrain them. He opens his mouth and the buzz of the crowd rises an octave. He pauses, his mouth still open, but no words come out. His hand dips, the palm now facing the ground, and then flicks outward towards the men in desperation.

The whole of Office Street now erupts in a collective outburst of anger, fuelled by the bitterness of betrayal and the prolonged tension induced by half a year without wages. The railings are rocked by a hundred hands forward back forward that's all it takes before the fence is down and scores of boots thunder into the pit yard. Cars are tossed over as if they were dinky toys, the sky is dark with falling rocks and the sound of splintering glass is everywhere.

Some one shouts 'no, that's the union office!,' and a picket, who is not from Easington, lowers his brick-filled hand and charges on into the pit yard leaving the windows of the union office unharmed.

The older men and the women stay in Office Street fearful. They are at one with the anger, they are gripped by the excitement of the moment and they strain to see what is happening now far across the yard.

Then they see beyond the men in the yard, by the corner of the time office, opposite the South shaft heapstead, rows of police forming up, helmeted, visors down truncheons in hand and shields on their arms. The pickets in the yard hesitate; rocks are thrown towards the ranks of the police. They jeer and motion to them to come forward.

Now there is the rhythmic beat of truncheons on shields. The familiar tribal sounds as the police hype themselves up.

Suddenly on command the ranks of the police burst forward, they sprint towards the young miners screaming. An instant reflex surges through the crowd in the pit yard and they turn like a wave on the nearby beach and race back in the direction of Office Street and towards the safety of the community.

The first wave bursts over the six foot wall on the east side of the main gate and into the street. Behind the wall fire extinguishers have been placed by the pickets. Others leap over the flattened railings on the west side.

The last are over the wall when one is caught astride the wall by three police from Gwent. For a moment he is held stationary as the momentum of his body forward is equally balanced by the arm of a policeman pulling him back. The picket strains to lever himself over the wall with his arms. There is a gasp from the crowd as his head is split by a maniacal blow from a truncheon and then there is a roar of three fire extinguishers blasting a white cloud of carbon dioxide into the faces of the police behind the wall and six pairs of hands drag the young miner off the wall and to the relative safety of Office Street.

Now the police re-group to charge into Office Street and the mass of pickets run for the safety of the pit rows, charging round both ends of the short terrace opposite the pit gates. Doors open and miners run through the houses into the back lanes. Once gaining the safety of the surrounding streets they stop and, hands on knees, struggle for breath. They turn and look back towards the colliery in disbelief.

Their is to be no repeat performance the next day. The police erect road blocks and the village is sealed off. Miners, or any who

may be miners, no longer are allowed to exercise their right to freedom of movement.

For the duration of the strike the vast majority of Easingtons men remained loyal to the union and they marched back to work as one body. After the return to work in 1985 few doubted that Easington was safe well into the 21st century. When in May of that year the NCB announced the closure of Horden colliery fears were expressed that if Horden was to close it would in time threaten the survival of Easington and the other nearby collieries. In Durham the pressure of the subterranean water builds up from the west of the county, pushing its way eastward. To relieve this pressure a number of pumping stations throughout the county pump water out of abandoned mineworkings. The cost of this operation is shared as an operational cost between the collieries that benefit. As collieries close a higher proportion of the costs fall on remaining pits.

On top of this financial penalty worries were that as Horden's workings flooded this water

Photo: Keith Pattison

Easington miners march back to work after 1984/85 strike

Easington colliery with new British Coal flag flying 1989

would find its way through the strata into Murton, Dawdon and Easington. By 1991, after the closure of Seaham, Dawdon and Murton, Easington was virtually bearing the full cost of the pumping operation alone.

As the post-strike race for survival accelerated production was concentrated in the J and G seams. Easington suffered from the same pressures that were now facing all mines: falling manpower and ever-rising production targets. Output per man-shift soared, but to no avail. To the horror of the whole country this efficient and productive unit appeared on Mr Heseltine's list and was closed in April 1993.

The mine was closed but the old pit had one last attempt to claim a life.

Barry Reay an Assistant engineer, Norman Walker and Kit Stout were working at the bottom of the old West pit making preparations to plug the shaft. Over the years a large amount of debris and slurry had accumulated in the disused shaft and this was being cleared by Kit and Norman. Kit was working

Demolition work begins 1993

in the shaft when the debris piled around the shaft edges suddenly collapsed burying Kit.

While Barry rushed to the telephone to summon help Norman frantically dug with his bare hands to reach Kit. Kit was fast losing consciousness when Norman felt the leather belt around Kit's waist several feet below. Bracing himself Norman held fast to Kit's belt. Then, straining every muscle in his body, he lifted Kit until his head was above the suffocating mixture of stone and slurry.

It was the last act of heroism in a pit that over its 94 years of life had seen its fair share.

Greenside colliery after re-opening in 1901

GREENSIDE COLLIERY

Greenside is situated in the Pennine foothills overlooking the Tyne valley in the most northerly area of the Durham coalfield. The collieries of Stella and Ryton are named as early as 1590 by the Lord Mayor of London in a complaint made to Lord Burleigh about the price the coal traders of Newcastle were charging for coal.

Documents of 1692 refer to a Stella Grand Lease colliery, Oak Tree Pit working the Grand Lease in the Main Coal seam.

The Grand Lease was a royalty given to Queen Elizabeth 1 by the Bishop of Durham. Elizabeth then transferred it to the Earl of Leicester who in turn transferred it to the Newcastle Hostmen, a society which had been granted the sole right to load coal on any part of the river Tyne. The

93

Hostmen had the power to fix the price of coal and it was this practice which had attracted the wrath of the Lord Mayor of London in 1590.

In 1785 reference is made to a Grand Lease colliery, Oak Tree pit, on Mr. Londridge's estate.

In 1795 <u>Borings and Sinkings</u> refer in separate entries to two sinkings 100 yds apart both called the A pit and owned by Mathias Dunn and Co. Although different depths and seams are given for the shafts it is almost certain that both records refer to the same shaft. Other records refer to an explosion at Greenside A pit killing six men in 1797.

The land on which the A pit was sunk was leased from the Silvertop family. In 1805 a dispute arose over the lease and resulted in the Silvertop family sinking a new shaft, the B pit, on the Silvertop estate, in direct competition to the A pit. The shaft was sunk to the five quarter seam at a depth of 361ft. The men who undertook the sinking were James Hall, the father of the famous mining engineer T.Y. Hall, and George Silvertop, who wrote himself into history when he became the unofficial emissary to the exiled Napoleon Bonaparte.

The B pit was never a large concern and employed around 29 men selling its coal to local smithies and farms.

After 1808 the owners of Greenside colliery sunk a second shaft, the C shaft, 350ft to the Tilly seam. This pit was a failure and earned the nick name the Folly pit.

In 1825 Mathias Dunn died, and as a result of a dispute over his will, the colliery was taken over

Greenside B pit with members of the Wilkinson family c. 1900

Gantry being built to screens, Greenside colliery

by the Silvertop family and closed. The mines equipment was sold off by Dunn's creditors and the shaft was back filled with sand.

By 1834 the Folly pit was closed and all that remained was the B pit.

In 1840 the viewer at the B pit was a man called Robert Simpson who in 1869 acquired the pit himself. By 1870 the mine's workforce was a mere ten men, four of whom belonged to the Wilkinson family.

Greenside colliery remained little more than a hole in the ground until 1901 when it received the attention of the Stella Coal Company. This company had been formed in 1839 and had on its board such giants of the industry as T.Y. Hall, John Buddle and Addison L. Potter who were later joined by several members of the Simpson family.

It was decided to reopen the old A pit and to widen its shaft to a diameter of 14ft. The depth of the shaft remained unchanged but an inset was made at the Brockwell seam as its main drawing level at 468ft. A boiler-house was built for a steam winder and after redevelopment the colliery drew its first coals in 1904. The close proximity of the N.E.R main line to the colliery required a gantry to be built over the railway to take the colliery's tubs to the screens. The tubs were pulled to the screens by ponies before a rope haulage system was installed.

A new line was laid from the screens to the nearby Stargate colliery connecting Greenside with the Stella network and the staithes at Dunstan.

This new development closed the B pit but the C pit, the old Folly, was to be utilised as a back shaft for Stargate colliery.

With the development of the mine the village of

Greenside grew and in 1925 a miners' welfare was built.

Greenside colliery was typical of Durham north-west pits. The seams were thin but the quality was good, a combination that did not lend itself to mechanisation, and at Greenside hand hewing and hand putting was the principal method of extraction.

After the General Strike of 1926 the Stella Coal company embarked on a programme of modernisation and electrified the mine, introducing main and tail and endless haulage systems. In the five quarter seam, which at three-feet-six inches was the thickest seam, coal cutters were introduced to undercut the coal. This new impetus to production helped the colliery break its production record by producing 380,000 tons of coal and employing 700 men.

The 1930s brought the inevitable decline in the colliery from which it had not recovered by the time it was nationalised in 1947. The NCB made some attempt to mechanise the Ruler and the Crow Coal seams with little success.

In 1953 the Phoenix drift was driven into the Main Coal and the Old Five Quarter to reach an area of coal isolated from the main shafts by faults. The drift was 200yds long and dipped at a gradient of one-in-eight.

Short wall faces were developed where coal was hewed with pneumatic picks and hand filled onto a belt face conveyer. The coal was

Photo: J. Carrick   *Coming off shift, Greenside colliery 1936*

Face workers, Crow seam
Greenside 1936
Photo: J. Carrick

Man riding set, Ruler seam
Greenside colliery 1936
Photo: J.Carrick

moved on belts to a loading point where it was loaded into tubs. At bank the tubs were tipped into a large hopper from which the coal was filled into lorries to transport it to the consumer.

A total of eight faces were developed in two seams, 24 men working on each face.

Throughout its entire life the Phoenix drift suffered the old Durham problem, the constant hazard of ancient and unmarked workings.

By the 1960s the colliery was losing money and in an attempt to cut costs the rail link was closed and all the colliery's coal was transported by road. In 1964 the NCB announced the closure of the drift when dwindling reserves added to its inefficiency. The NCB gave the same reason to close the main colliery on July 23 1966.

Local people have become somewhat sceptical of the NCB's estimation of the colliery's reserves in view of the scale of the opencast mining that has prevailed in the Ryton area since the closure.

Greenside colliery at closure

MAINSFORTH COLLIERY

The village of Mainsforth is situated close to Ferryhill between the old A1 and the new A1M. The origins of the Mainsforth colliery date from 1873 when two shafts, the East and the West, were sunk 270ft to the Five Quarter seam. These workings were short-lived and by 1877 the mine was abandoned and the shafts used as a rubbish dump. The exact cause of the mine's demise is not clear and has been attributed both to the slackness in the coal trade due to the end of the Franco-Prussian war and the inundation of the pit by water.

It was not until 23 years later that the site attracted the attention of the Carlton Iron Company who, having acquired the lease, re-excavated the abandoned shafts and de-watered the workings.

Mainsforth colliery c. 1915

The company then proceeded to widen and deepen the two shafts. The East pit, which was both the downcast and the coal drawing shaft, was deepened to the Harvey seam where an inset was constructed at 850ft. In anticipation of a return of the previous water problems the shaft was deepened a further 40ft to provide a sump, and when complete this shaft had a finished diameter of 14ft six inches.

The West shaft, the upcast, with a finished diameter of 14ft, was also deepened to the Harvey with an inset at 850ft, but in this case the sump was only 15ft deep. From the bottom of this shaft the owners bored down to prove the Busty and Brockwell seams.

Metal headgears of a lattice construction were erected over each shaft and the cages were powered by twin-tandem horizontal steam engines built by Thornhill and Warham Ltd. The coal shaft winder was capable of raising 12.5 tons 850ft in 22 seconds.

The coal was graded at the surface on picking belt screens, and transported via a new 1/2 mile branch line to the Stockton-Ferryhill railway. The junction was one mile south of Ferryhill.

As the construction of the new mine neared completion the company's only other mine East Howle, was consumed by fire. The fire started in one of the shafts and quickly spread to the surface buildings, eventually destroying the heapsteads of both shafts. As luck would have it no one was killed as a result of the fire but all the pit ponies that were underground were overcome by the fumes and perished.

Mainsforth colliery drew its first coal in the December of 1905 and by 1910 was producing a quarter of a million tons of coal and fireclay a year. A decade later this production had doubled and the mine was employing 2,000 men.

In 1923 the Carlton Iron Company was absorbed by Dorman and Long Ltd. of Middlesbrough, which was already the biggest steel-making company in the area and was turning its attention to the acquisition of coal mines. This new company installed new single-reduction helical gears in the West pit winder, enabling it to ride men from all the insets in the shaft.

The abandoned shafts of the Bishop Middleham colliery lay a mile-and-a-half north-east of Mainsforth colliery. These shafts had been sunk in 1864, 480ft to the Low main seam. They had been worked intermittently until some time shortly before the turn of the century. The new company now planned to deepen the shafts to the Harvey seam at 684ft and to work the area as a unit independent of Mainsforth colliery.

The development of a power plant was planned but the work on this project was interrupted by the 1926 strike.

In an effort to keep the pits working during the dispute the company imported blackleg labour from Teesside. Each day a train transporting the blacklegs would arrive at Ferryhill station, where they were taken by police escort the 200 yards to the pit. The route was regularly lined with the miners and their families hurling insults and abuse. On more than one occasion the police baton-charged the crowd and many local people sustained injuries.

One of the miners many grievances was the way the management counted the tubs. The pit was known as a 21-score pit, as they had to produce 21 tubs to be paid for a score (20). The extra tub was claimed by the owners to pay for the Royalty.

After the return to work in November 1926 the company continued the development of the mine and completed the building of the new power-house. This power-house was installed with two Lancaster dyno generators built by Bellis and Morcom Ltd. These generators were driven from

Mainsforth colliery c.1920

the exhaust steam of the engines which drove the winders and fan. Transformers and cables were installed to take the electricity down the West pit.

At Bishop Middleham the deepening of the shafts recommenced and by 1928 the Harvey had been reached. No sooner was the Harvey reached than it was engulfed by an explosion that mercifully claimed no lives, although several men were severely injured.

In 1929 Mainsforth colliery was furnished with the luxury of pit-head baths, the upkeep of which was shared between the men and management. Underground access was gained to the Busty No.

1 and No. 2 seams by means of a one-in-six drift 300yds long. The drift was served by a 300hp hauler and the coal was extracted by both bord-and-pillar and long-wall methods. In early 1931 the company experimented with short retreating walls using belt conveyers on the faces, with a considerable degree of success.

The faces were won by driving two gates 12ft wide and a distance of 33 yards apart using Hardy Header coal cutters. When the gates had reached a distance of 360 yards a face was driven between the two gates, on which a conveyer belt was installed. The coal was then extracted from the

Two views of Mainsforth colliery 1930s with new dry washer and screens

face working back out-bye. These retreating faces proved a great success.

The porous limestone and sand beds that overlay the coal measures in this part of County Durham supplied the mine with abnormal quantities of run-of-the-mine water, to such a degree that the mine was selling it to the Durham County Water Board from a specially built waterworks situated just north of the colliery. What could not be sold was diverted into the river Stell.

By the 1930s, despite the depression the colliery was producing 740,000 tons of coal and employing 2,054 men. In 1936 the company opened the Bishop Middleham shafts for riding men and materials, and they became known as the back shafts.

In the late thirties the company constructed a dry spiral washer which was capable of handling all Mainsforth's production as well as some coal imported from other collieries. At this time the Bottom Hutton seam and the Brockwell seam were opened. The Brockwell seam at 1,122ft was the deepest seam to be worked at Mainsforth, and both seams were entered by the well-tested method of drifting, on this occasion from the Harvey seam.

By the time the pit was nationalised in 1947 it was second only to the nearby Dean and Chapter

Mainsforth colliery 1950s after winding set was change

103

Bishop Middleham shaft 1956

colliery as the largest and most important in Durham's central coalfield.

The first benefit nationalisation brought to the miners of Mainsforth was the bus which the new administration provided to ferry the men between the Bishop Middleham shafts and the baths at the main colliery. Previously the men had to make the mile-and-a half journey on foot.

In 1953 the prospects for the colliery looked bright when the NCB announced a restructuring programme for Mainsforth's underground workings and the exploitation of two new seams, the Low Main and the Main Coal in the higher measures. Fully mechanised faces were to be introduced and a new inset was built at the shaft at the Low Main level to take the coals to bank.

Some attempt was also made to work the Brass Thill seam but it proved deeper than was at first thought and its quality was poor. The seam was soon abandoned.

The West shaft heapstead was rebuilt, increasing its capacity for man-riding, and a new electric winder was installed.

At the East shaft a new winder house was built, opposite the old steam winder house, to house the East pit's new electric winder. New stay legs were added to the headgear as the direction of the pull on the pulley wheel was reversed by the winder's new position. New cages were installed capable of handling the new one-ton mine cars and by 1958 all the reconstruction plans were completed. Bishop Middleham's shafts were then closed as they were now deemed to be surplus to requirements.

On Friday August 30 1963 Mainsforth colliery suffered an explosion, the cause of which was probably the strangest on record.

A deputy, John Hamilton, and an overman, John Bowdon, were preparing to go underground to carry out the statutory inspections. A thunderstorm was brewing and they noticed a flash in the overhead cables at the pit-head baths. Both men descended by the West shaft and on getting out of the cage they both smelt what seemed like burning rubber, not unlike the smell of a burned-out motor. On the way in-bye Hamilton and Bowdon split up, each to inspect his own district. When Hamilton reached the Fifth North District he was confronted by a scene of total devastation.

The water ranges had been ruptured and water was gushing everywhere. The arch roof girders were bent and twisted and in some places the roof had collapsed. A row of tubs had been lifted up by the force of the explosion and concertinad into the roof.

Fortunately it was the pit holidays and no men had been working in the district. Violent as the explosion had been it had been confined to the district by the stone-dust barriers. These loose planks of wood onto which is piled stone dust had done the job they were designed to do. When the explosion occurred the planks were blown over and the stone dust cloud created an inert path across which the fire ball could not pass to ignite more coal dust.

The inquiry into the accident concluded that lightning had struck the mine's power supply and a high charge of lightning had passed through the

Mainsforth colliery 1968

main supply down the shaft and into the cable supplying the district with electrical power. The charge had tried to find a path to earth through the earthing strap on a transformer. Because the bolt on the strap was loose a spark was generated which caused the explosion.

As the men in the Durham No. 4 area were still on holiday miners had to be bused in from the coastal mines to put the district back into operation.

This unlikely tale was often repeated to apprentice electricians to warn them of the importance of maintaining the earth straps on electrical apparatus in the best of condition.

Mainsforth was now to suffer problems, as one face after another hit geological faults. To add to the problems the rate at which the mine was making water increased and one face in the Low Main was producing 4,000 gals per minute.

On the weekend of September 28 1968 No.11 face in the Low Main seam was inundated with water in such quantities that the pumps could not cope, and it took several weeks before the water was brought under control. This was bad news indeed for the future of the mine but once again, mercifully the miners of Mainsforth had cheated death by conveniently being on holiday when the disaster struck.

The pumping continued for another two months without making much progress. As time passed the prospects seemed more and more gloomy and men were being transferred away from the colliery.

Had the demand for coal been greater the pit might have survived, but this was the 1960s, and the age of cheap oil. The colliery closed on December 6 1968. Those men who remained in the industry transferred to other pits. For the rest this was to be the end of their mining careers.

THE SOUTH MOOR GROUP OF COLLIERIES
THE CHARLEY, HEDLEY, LOUISA, MORRISON OLD, MORRISON BUSTY, WILLIAM PITS AND SHIELD ROW DRIFT.

In areas where mining has been intense and protracted, the history of collieries in close proximity to each other become interwoven and indeed inseparable. This is the case with the South Moor group of collieries.

The South Moor royalty covered an area of 4,000 acres on the eastern flank of the Pennine foothills in North-west Durham. On this undulating landscape the villages of South Moor, Oxhill, Quaking Houses, New Kyo, Craghead and Holmside and the small towns of Stanley and Annfield Plain owe their development entirely to the coal seams that lay below.

Coal was commercially mined in the area as far back as 1726, when one member of the Grand Allies, a Newcastle merchant by the name of Thomas Ord, worked a colliery known as Ords Main Colliery. There were others: The Knap, Oxhill, Broom, Edge, West Shield Row, the Pea (some times referred to as Hedleys Pit), The Fox and the Adam. This profusion of collieries in the area was to a large extent a result of the still

Photo: G. Muncaster

Morrison North and South pits 1890

primitive state of the mines of that time. The workings of each individual concern could not be extensive due to the rudimentary nature of the ventilation. At a time when mines were powered by the muscle of man and beast the coal was drawn up the shafts by a horse-powered gin, and once at bank was loaded into carts and hauled to the South Moor Wagon way.

By 1800 the royalty and the mines within it had been acquired by William Bell and his partners, one of whom was the locomotive engineer William Hedley. The Hedley family were destined to play a prominent role in the history of the region's mines. They distiguished themselves as progressive employers for their time.

In 1839 these partners sunk a shaft which was called the West Craghead pit at Map Reference NZ 1907 5096. In 1839 the site of this mine was still known as South Moor but the village that was to be built on the site was given the name Quaking Houses, and the pit became known as the New South Moor pit.

The shaft was sunk 461 ft to the Hutton seam and a wagon way was laid to Oxhill, where a stationary steam engine was built. A similar engine at the pit lowered the full wagons of coal down the incline to a landing close to the Stanley Burn. At this point the wagons were uncoupled and attached to the rope of the Oxhill engine and hauled up to Oxhill. Having reached the summit of the incline the wagons were transferred to the Stanhope and Tyne Railway, (later to become the Pontop and Shields Railway). The first coal left the mine on July 25 1841.

To a miner of these times a job on the Oxhill standing engines, compared with one down the

Charley pit 1910

William pit Quaking Houses 1910

pit, must have seemed an inviting prospect. However, with boiler technology still in its infancy, working alongside one of these early engines could be compared with working on the lip of an active volcano, as the events of October 25 1845 were to prove.

On this fateful day the Oxhill boiler exploded, killing, Thomas Potts immediately. Four others were scalded, two of whom, Dan Tempest and George Armstrong, died later of their injuries.

Again in 1853 this engine exploded, killing the engine wright Thomas Clark.

In 1845 a second pit was sunk 3/4 of a mile south east of the William pit 310ft to the Brass Thill seam. This pit was first named the Quaking House pit. It was later renamed the West Shield Row pit before it finally became known as the Charley Pit. Coals from this pit were lowered to South Moor village, then hauled up to Oxhill.

On the site chosen for the Charley pit there still

remained a much older shaft over which was built a stone building. The shaft was furnished with a series of landings at regular intervals connected by ladders. This shaft stood as a grim reminder of those, horrific times when women and children would carry the coals to bank in baskets balanced on their heads.

A brickworks was to be built beside Charley pit and in 1863 the partners had embarked upon the sinking of the Louisa shaft, named after the wife of William Bell, which was sited in Stanley's front street. The shaft was sunk 540 ft to the Low Main seam and was connected by a direct route to the Pontop and Shields line for the disposal of its coals. This new sinking in effect rendered the New South Moor pit unnecessary and it was subsequently closed.

The Charley pit's coals were now also diverted via the Louisa, making the Oxhill engine redundant.

Together the Charley and the Louisa Pits became known as the South Moor Colliery.

In 1869 the company concentrated on the Annfield Plain part of the royalty, where it undertook the sinking of two shafts which were named Morrison, after one of the partners, Jas Morrison. The first of these two shafts was the North pit, which was sunk 600ft to the Hutton seam and the second the South pit sunk to a similar depth but drawing from the upper measures.

A double battery of coke ovens was built to process the coking coal on site.

Coal from the mine was cleared via a branch line 1 1/2 miles long to the Pontop and Shields line. The junction of these two lines was close to where the Ox Inn at Oxhill stands today.

As the company expanded it sunk a second shaft alongside the Louisa shaft 530ft to the Low Main seam although it was to draw coal from the Shield Row inset at 250. The new shaft became known as the Shield Row or the Louisa New shaft, while its sister shaft was renamed the Louisa Old shaft. The Old shaft was now widened to 14 ft and deepened to the Victoria seam at 1,050 ft, but because of the thinning of the coal seams at this depth and the disturbed nature of the ground the shaft was eventually back-filled to the Hutton inset at 640 ft.

After the sinking of the Louisa New pit the coals from the Charley shaft were transported underground to be drawn at the Louisa pit.

The company also drove two drifts from the valley bottom, near Quaking Houses, close to the Stanley Burn into the Shield Row seam, to work the coal under Langley Moor. These were known as the Shield Row drifts (not to be confused with the Shield Row drift of Sacriston, see volume 1)

The Shield Row drift in effect consisted of a North and a South drift. The coal from these workings was drawn at the Louisa New shaft but before the coal tubs could arrive at their eventual destination they first had to be hauled out of the South into the North drift, on to the Charley shaft, and from the Charley shaft to the Louisa. The fan house for the South drifts can still be seen today at Quaking Houses, where it is used as a lock-up garage.

In 1885 the partners decided to sink a further shaft. Originally the site for the sinking was chosen at the old wagon-landing close to the site of the Oxhill stationary engine. Part of their plan was to re-open the old line. It was, however, finally decided that it would be less expensive to sink the new shaft just north-east of the closed New South Moor pit. This shaft was 566ft in depth to the Low Main seam and was called the Hedley pit after William Hedley Senior. Records show that a second upcast shaft was developed at about the same time as the Hedley sinking, although it is not clear whether this was a new sinking or if an old shaft was recommissioned. A model of the

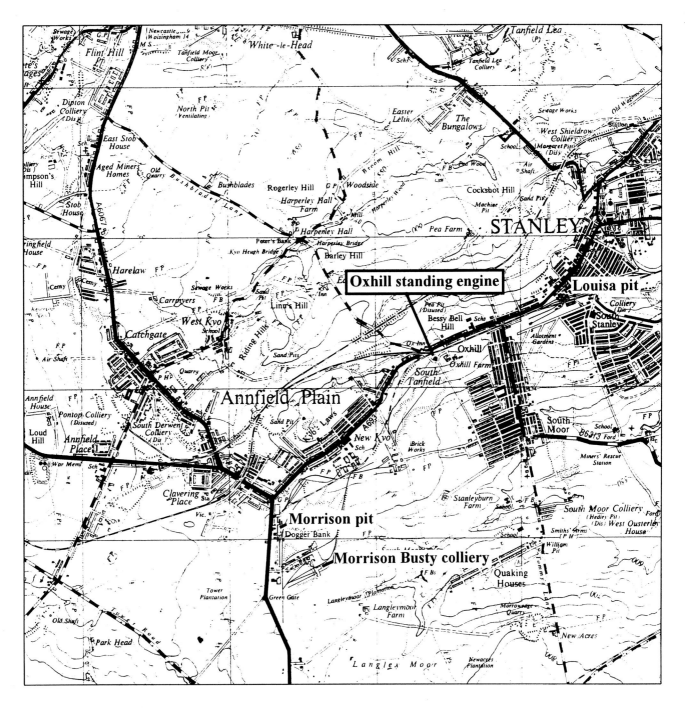

unusual ventilation system of these shafts is now exhibited at Newcastle Science Museum.

A double-track endless-rope tub-line was constructed to transport the coals from this new sinking to the screens at Louisa colliery.

All these shafts now collectively made up the South Moor colliery. and as all were drawing coal it was decided in 1893 to sink a further shaft as a central ventilation shaft. This ventilation shaft was sited at the Charley pit and was sunk 460ft to the Hutton seam. It was fitted with a 30ft diameter Waddle fan and with the exception of the Shield Row drift this shaft superseded all the previous ventilation systems.

In 1894 a tragic accident occurred in the Louisa Old shaft. Two men, John Barron and William Neal, were ascending to bank when a large stone fell from the side of the shaft, striking the cage. John died immediately from the impact of the stone while William was knocked out of the cage and plunged to the bottom of the shaft where he was fatally injured.

As the 19th century drew to a close the influence of the Hedley family increased and a new company was floated called South Moor Collieries Ltd.

In 1898, in order to expand, the new company reopened the disused New South Moor colliery, which was again renamed the William pit, this time after William Hedley junior. Local miners gave it their own name, and it was always referred to as the Billy pit. It is said that the chuffing noise

The Charley pit 1910, giant waddle fan to right

Photo G. Muncaster

Sinking of the Morrison Busty shafts 1923

of its vertical steam winder dominated the life of the village.

The tub line at the Hedley pit was extended to the William pit to transport the coal of the re-opened colliery.

In 1900 the company began the modernisation of its mines and embarked on a building programme that was to include the construction of a new village for its miners at Quaking Houses. The bricks for this development were conveyed from the brick-works at the Charley pit by an aerial flight. Although this flight was dismantled probably before 1920 traces of it remain to this day.

In the course of the modernisation both the North and the South pits at the Morrison were completely rebuilt. Underground coal cutters were introduced and many pit ponies were replaced when new rope haulage systems were introduced. Although the use of electrical power was increasing in popularity at many collieries the group remained heavily dependent on steam power.

This complex of shafts and drifts collectively known as South Moor colliery was being worked effectively as one unit. If the miners were gaining access to an area of coal from one shaft and the workings progressed towards another shaft in the group they would descend by the second shaft as soon as it became more convenient.

During the First World War the colliery suffered

as all others from a shortage of manpower and as a consequence it was decided to close the Charley pit. Coal-work never returned to the Charley pit although the fan shaft was to remain in operation for many years to come.

After the end of hostilities in Europe and the return to peace-time production the South Moor company took a long hard look at its operation. The collection of shafts that had served their purpose well were now deemed to be overmanned and not best capable of exploiting the six virgin seams of coal that lay below the Hutton seam.

An ambitious plan was conceived to mine the lower seams for the whole of the royalty, with the

exception of an area around Craghead, from a new mine that would be sunk just 500 yds south of the Morrison shafts. This new pit would be known as the Morrison Busty colliery, and the first sods of the new shafts the East and the West were cut in June 1923.

The sinking was conducted by J. Denham and Co. of Bishop Auckland. Temporary headgears were at first erected over the shafts and by 1925 both shafts had bottomed out to the Brockwell seam at 780ft. Each shaft was lined with a nine-inch-thick ring of concrete and bricked out throughout its entire length with a nine-inch lining of bricks. The finished diameter of the shafts was

Hedley pit 1910

Louisa pit 1920

an ample 22ft. The East shaft was made the downcast shaft and had insets at the Towneley, the Busty and the Brockwell seams for coal drawing. The West pit, the upcast shaft for the new colliery, had insets made at all the seams, although in fact it only ever drew coal from the Brockwell.

The one puzzling factor in this most modern of sinkings was the apparent mistrust the company had in electrical power. Electricity had by now a proven record at many collieries yet the owners insisted on steam power for both the winding engines. There was some electrical equipment at the shaft bottoms but in-bye the coal cutters were powered by compressed air.

The two Robey-built winding engines were housed on either side of the power house, which supplied what electrical energy was required by the company.

Once the main steel headgears had been erected above the shafts massive single-decked cages each capable of holding six 12 cwt tubs were installed.

At bank the tubs ran along a gantry to the tippler house and screens.

Ventilation was provided by a steam driven Sirrocco fan with an electrically driven Siroco as a back-up.

The new mine was planned to employ 2,000 men and boys and it was hoped that it would produce 3,000 tons of coal per day.

On January 3 1925, the Hedley Coal Company merged with South Moor Collieries Ltd. to form Holmside and South Moor Collieries Ltd. This

115

Morrison Busty colliery 1925.

Fan house under construction Morrison Busty 1923

Completed fan house, 1924

116

company was to distinguish itself as the only large Durham company not to join that unholy alliance 'The Durham Coal Owners Association'.

While the sinking of the new colliery progressed the owners and miners of the British coal industry became locked in a trial of strength that was to culminate in the long strike of 1926 and delay the raising of coal from this new development until 1927.

In the dark days that followed the 1926 conflict, relations between owners and men were filled with bitter recriminations and victimisation was rife throughout the county. Holmside and South Moor Collieries Ltd, however was regarded as a progressive employer. In co-operation with the union a welfare and a hospital were built for the miners and their families and the first rescue station in the county was established at Hustledown.

In 1929 the colliery was engulfed in a catastrophe when a fire caused by an acetylene lamp engulfed the main haulage road connecting

Hedley pit, 1930

the Morrison North shaft and the Louisa. For a month the raging fire laid the Morrison Old, Louisa, William and Hedley pits idle before it was finally brought under control. Once the fire was out, fire stoppings were constructed and until the day the area was finally abandoned it had to be closely monitored and patrolled as there was a constant danger of a spontaneous rekindling of the fire.

In the history of all pits, death and heroism play a prominent role, and it would be impossible to record all such instances. On September 29 1930, however, an incident occured at the Hedley pit that epitomised the bravery that had become a natural part of a miner's nature.

A hewer, Fred Beaumont, became entombed by a serious roof fall. All 19 of his workmates refused to leave him to his fate, and, shoring the unstable roof as best they could, they worked towards the trapped man. The rescuers were themselves trapped when the roof collapsed behind them, but confident that others were coming to their aid continued to advance towards where Fred Beaumont was trapped. No words can describe the horror and fear of such occasions. Yet these men worked skilfully, using every ounce of their combined strength to hack a path to their entombed comrade. Their labours were rewarded when Beaumont was eventually freed, and all survived the ordeal.

All 19 men were awarded the Edward medal for bravery by the King at a ceremony in 1932.

Photo: G. Muncaster

North and South pits Morrison colliery, 1930s

In 1932 witherite (barium carbonate) was discovered at the Morrison North pit in sufficient quantities to be economically mined. This made the Morrison pit and Settlingstones in Northumberland the only two pits in Britain to have discovered workable reserves of witherite.

In 1933 a further shaft was sunk for the purpose of riding the men who were to extract this unexpected bounty. The mineral was brought to bank via the North shaft.

In 1942 the company finally began the electrification of the mine underground at the Morrison Busty pit.

In 1943 the company began the rationalisation of the older shafts in the group and designated the Louisa pit as the only pit to draw the coals from the upper measures. Underground locomotives of the Rushton type, the first in County Durham to be used for coal transport, were introduced to haul the coal from the other shafts to the Louisa.

Once the Morrison Busty had been sunk to extract the lower seams it was understood that the other pits would have a limited life-span, and in 1945 the old Morrison South pit was closed, followed one year later by the Hedley pit, whose reserves were then worked from the Louisa shaft. Now, just to confuse the local historians the Shield Row shaft at the Louisa Pit was renamed the Hedley shaft.

These changes rendered the old tub line connecting the William, Hedley and Louisa pit, redundant.

In 1946 German Ploughs were introduced into the Busty seam at the Morrison Busty colliery, making it the first colliery in Britain to experiment with this particular type of coal-cutting equipment.

Louisa colliery, 1940

Photo: G. Muncaster

Morrison Busty colliery in 1940s

The company scored another first when it constructed the first purpose-built medical centre with its own full-time nurse, Mrs Duary, an ex-RAF Nursing sister.

In 1947, only eight months after the Nationalisation of the mine the community was stunned by news of a terrible tragedy underground.

On August 22 1947, three deputies, W. Younger, J. Shanley, and H. Robinson were on fire-watch duty during the night shift. Their job was to carefully monitor the area sealed off after the 1929 fire. The original stoppings, built immediately after the fire had been relocated closer to where the seat of the fire had been, in order to allow an new area of coal to be worked. As there

was still evidence of heat being generated in the fire area the deputies were at pains to give the district a thorough examination.

In-bye, in the Fourth North district of the Hutton seam two miners, Minto and Westgarth, were beginning their shift and had reached the loading point 30yds from the coal face. They were stripping and preparing themselves for work when they heard a bang and were plunged into unconsciousness.

The three deputies were on their way in-bye from the Morrison North shaft. They reached the main road of the Low Main seam where they stopped to examine the fire stoppings. At 11.55pm they had just reached the fire station when they felt the air flow halt momentarily. Seconds later a rush of dust-laden air engulfed them. All knew immediately that somewhere in-bye an explosion had occurred.

Because of the nature of their duties the deputies were carrying flame-lamp detectors and a canary. They also had access to survival apparatus and were trained rescuers.

They turned and ran in the direction of the Morrison North shaft, towards the area which they thought was the seat of the explosion. On reaching the Fourth North district of the Hutton seam their fears were confirmed and Shanley returned to the Fourth Bankhead to relay the news to bank by telephone. Younger and Robinson entered the district, taking the canary with them. In front of them was a heavy brattice cloth which they found intact. Through the brattice they gained access to Straight East Gate where they could see a light straight ahead of them and could hear a moaning sound. They found Minto, 30yds on, alive but unconscious. Two others, Bailey and Talbot, were apparently dead.

Younger remained with Minto while Robinson returned out-bye to telephone for assistance and to bring a stretcher for the injured man. Meanwhile Younger made a further examination of Bailey and on finding him still alive, decided to go out-bye to meet Robinson returning with the stretcher and to send him for the survival apparatus.

When Robinson returned he had with him Shanley and the fore-overman John Hutchinson,

Photo: G. Muncaster

Rescue team at Hustledown Rescue Station 1920.

who had descended by the North shaft at midnight. Together they removed the three men from the Straight East Gate.

As they proceeded to examine the fume-laden district they discovered two drillers, Johnson and Kilgallon, unconscious but alive at the deputy's kist and were able to bring them out into the fresh air. Later at the same spot they were able to rescue the deputy Estell, mercifully still alive but again unconscious.

By the time the first rescue team arrived at 1.30 a.m. five of the dead had been retrieved from the South Heading and a further four dead bodies had been located in the Second East loading gate.

The rescue team quickly extinguished several smouldering fires and retrieved the remainder of the dead men. In all 21 had perished.

A detailed examination of the district left the Government Inspector in no doubt as to the cause of the accident. Throughout the district their was evidence of smoked cigarettes, and even at the deputy's kist cigarette ends and spent matches were found.

Near to the loading point, a whole cigarette and a partly damage whole cigarette were found alongside a used match. It was here that the inspector concluded that the explosion had been caused by a miner attempting to light a cigarette.

To the miners of today, over four decades after all mines became 'safety lamp mines', it seems inconceivable that any miner would take such risk with his life and that of his workmates. It has to be remembered however that the use of naked flame lamps, like the acetylene lamp that started the 1929 fire, and in some cases even candles, were still widely used in the mines in the West of Durham.

In fact the Morrison Old pit was not itself a safety lamp mine, but a mixed lamp mine, i.e., safety lamp restrictions were only in force in parts of the mine, creating the situation where miners who could smoke underground mixed at some point in their shift with those working in restricted areas.

The inspector's report states;

'It is doubtful if safety lamps were legally required in any part of this mine, but in any event Section 35 of the Act was applied in its entirety to all sections in which safety lamps were in use, including the Fourth North Districts, as a voluntary precaution by management..''

It is not hard to see how such ambiguity could lead to a complacent attitude to smoking in the pit that was clearly shared not just by the men but the very deputies whose duty it was to enforce the restrictions.

The inspector concludes:

'.....I attribute this lack of discipline in the 4th North District revealed by the explosion to have been the consequential effect of "mixed light" conditions'.

The deputies Younger, Shanley and Robinson and the overman Hutchinson were all awarded the Edward medal for their part in the rescue and a trust fund for the relief of the families of the dead men collected £25,260.

In the wake of this tragedy the management proceeded with the modernisation of the mine. The old vertical steam winder at the William pit was replaced by a small electric winder and was only retained as an escape route in the event of the failure of the Louisa shaft.

The production of witherite at the Morrison North pit was discontinued and the pit was electrified underground.

By 1951 production ceased at the Shield Row drift and this unit was closed.

By the mid 1950s a new washer was being constructed at the Morrison Busty which had the

Photo: G. Muncaster

South Moor St. Johns Ambulance Cadets, William Younger Officer on right

capacity to process the coal from all the group's pits.

While the washer was under construction at the surface, underground the mining engineering firms of RB Bolton and Anderson Boyes were co-operating in the development of the first drum shearer. A face was installed in the 4th East, Main South district as an experimental face where the new machine could be tested and developed. The machine was mounted on an armoured conveyer and was hauled up the face by a hydraulic winch housed in the main gate. Picks mounted on a large steel drum revolved in the coal seam tearing out the coal and screwing it on to the armoured conveyer. The success of this machine was to transform the production of coal throughout the coalfields of Britain in the decades that lay ahead.

1958 saw the start of the electrification of the Morrison Busty Pit winders. First the West pit was converted, followed by the East pit a year later.

In the same year the final rationalisation of the upper measures of the group's pits was to take place. A spiral drop staple shaft was sunk at the old Morrison North pit between the Hutton seam and the Towneley. All the coal still produced at the old Morrison North and the Louisa was then taken to the staple in the Hutton seam and dropped to the Towneley, from where it was taken to the

Electricians putting coupler boxes on cables at Morrison Busty, 1947
Left to right: Les Harrison, Len Kay, Ivor Hobbs, Jack Harrison, Jimmy Gibson and Vender Hunter.
Photo G. Muncaster

124

Electrical staff at Morrison Busty, 1947.

Standing:
left, Albert Wilkinson,
(Asst. Electrical Engineer)
right, Norman Dixon,
(Electrical Engineer).
Seated top step:
left, Len Kay,
right, John Hubble (Bevin Boy)
Seated middle step:
left, Bill Wilson
right Bill ?.
Seated bottom step: Jeff Robertson.

Photo: G. Muncaster

Morrison Busty colliery, after closure

Morrison Busty East pit shaft and raised to bank.

By 1961 the old Morrison North had closed and work had started on the demolition of the Louisa screens and other buildings that were now surplus to requirements. By 1967 the Louisa colliery was itself closed and production was concentrated at the Morrison Busty pit.

Production lasted a further six years after which geological problems added to the depletion of the coal reserves.

The colliery closed on October 5 1973, 50 years after it had been sunk and bringing to an end 250 years of mining in the South Moor area.